D1288634

IT Management

Lionel Pilorget · Thomas Schell

IT Management

The art of managing IT based on a solid framework leveraging the company's political ecosystem

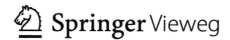

Lionel Pilorget
FHNW (Fachhochschule Nordwestschweiz)
Basel, Switzerland

Thomas Schell
consultare et discere
Lörrach, Germany

ISBN 978-3-658-19308-9   ISBN 978-3-658-19309-6 (eBook)
https://doi.org/10.1007/978-3-658-19309-6

Library of Congress Control Number: 2018936134

This Springer Vieweg imprint is published by Springer Nature, under the registered company Springer Fachmedien Wiesbaden GmbH
The registered company address is: Abraham-Lincoln-Str. 46, 65189 Wiesbaden, Germany

Contents

Abbreviations

API	Application Programming Interface
BCG	Boston Consulting Group
BCM	Business Continuity Management
BIA	Business Impact Analyse
BIL	Business Importance Level
BPMN	Business Process Model and Notation
BPO	Business Process Outsourcing
BSC	Balanced Scorecard
CEO	Chief Executive Officer
CFO	Chief Finance Officer
CI	Configuration Item
CIO	Chief Information Officer
CMDB	Configuration Management Database
CMMI	Capability Maturity Model Integration
COBIT®	Control Objectives for Information and related Technology
CSF	Critical Success Factor
CSI	Continuous Service Improvement
CSV	Computerized System Validation
EFQM	European Foundation for Quality Management
EQ	Emotional Quotient
ERP	Enterprise Resource Planning
FHNW	Fachhochschule Nordwestschweiz – University of Applied Sciences and Arts Northwestern Switzerland
FINMA	Swiss Financial Market Supervisory Authority
FTE	Full Time Equivalent
HR	Human Resources
HW	Hardware
IQ	Intellectual Quotient
ISACA	Information Systems Audit and Control Association
ISO	International Standards Organisation

IT	Information Technology
ITIL®	Information Technology Infrastructure Library
ITSM	Information Technology Service Management
KPI	Key Performance Indicator
MbO	Management by Objectives
NPV	Net Present Value
OLA	Operational Level Agreement
OS	Operating System
PC	Personal Computer
PDCA	Plan, Do, Check, Act (Deming Cycle)
PL	Project Leader
PoC	Proof of Concept
QA	Quality Assurance
R&D	Research & Development
RACI	Responsible – Accountable – Consulted – Informed
RCB	Release Control Board
RfC	Request for Change
ROI	Return on Investment
SaaS	Software as a Service
SACM	Service Asset and Configuration Management (ITIL® process)
SAP	System Applications Products
SIPOC	Supplier – Input – Process – Output – Customer
SL	Service Level
SLA	Service Level Agreement
SMART	Specific, Measurable, Attainable, Relevant and Timely
SMS	Service Management System
SPOC	Single Point Of Contact
STC	Steering Committee
SW	Software
SWIFT	Society for Worldwide Interbank Financial Telecommunication
SWOT	Strengths – Weaknesses – Opportunities – Threats
TMS	Team Management System
TOP	Technical Operation Procedure
UAT	User Acceptance Test
VIP	Very Important Person
WBS	Work Breakdown Structure

Introduction

1

Abstract

How to resolve the ostensible antagonism of relying on modern IT technologies whilst ensuring a sustainable future of a company? IT Management is certainly one of the key elements to achieve this.

"Classical" business management approaches apply by the way just as well to the management of IT. Moreover selected best practices to provide outstanding IT Management are also presented in this book.

Striking the right balance between perpetuation of internal knowledge and the management of external IT providers requires appropriate organizational measures for IT. And controlling IT expenditures and limiting the dependency on critical suppliers remain main tasks of the Head of IT.

The idea of writing a book about IT management was born when setting up lessons for a master study called "IT Management and Cloud Computing" at the FHNW (Fachhochschule Nordwestschweiz) in Switzerland. It appeared useful to find a way to explain the different aspects of IT management and to give an overview of current theories and business practices. Especially the gap between "*how IT management should work*" and "*how reality is*" needed to be reflected in order to provide a realistic start to the students.

Thus, the guiding principle of the book is to highlight the relationships between the different aspects of IT management and their ineluctable interdependencies.

This book aims at a pedagogical approach. This explains the large number of 126 figures included, since a picture is worth a thousand words. This will enable an easy and quick

© Springer Fachmedien Wiesbaden GmbH, part of Springer Nature 2018
L. Pilorget, T. Schell, *IT Management*,
https://doi.org/10.1007/978-3-658-19309-6_1

understanding of the topics presented. Moreover, some exercises are included. Also questions, which allow to reflect on typical situations concerning IT management within companies, are provided for the sake of a practical approach to the subjects.

The following boxes will indicate exercises and questions.

Exercises

Give your definition of IT management and the different aspects to be considered:

...

...

Questions

1. Do you have any question about the book?
2. Is the intention of the writers clear?
3. What do you expect when reading the book?

Additionally, some check lists are set out. They are recognizable with the following box:

Check List

a. ...

b. ...

c. ...

The book is divided into seven chapters which correspond to the elements used to define the IT management practices, as observed within companies (Fig. 1.1):

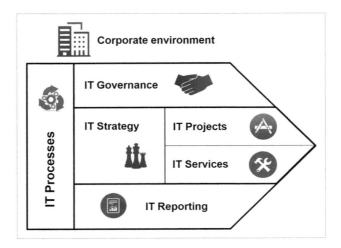

Fig. 1.1 Building the home of IT

Each topic is presented in a dedicated chapter. At the beginning of each chapter, the scope and the corresponding educational objectives are listed. This allows to get a short overview of all matters included in this book.

The current chapter aims at:

- adhering to the guiding principles of the book
- defining IT management
- understanding the main topics of IT management
- understanding the relationships between company needs and IT suppliers
- knowing the theory of make-or-buy decisions
- building an own opinion concerning the outsourcing of IT services

1.1   Definition of IT Management

The first question that should be asked when dealing with IT management is its definition. An elementary solution is to define "IT" and then "management" in order to get a definition of "IT management" (Fig. 1.2). The problem is that both areas are quite broad.

Following definitions will apply:

- **IT**: use of any technology including computers, storage, networking and other physical devices, infrastructure and processes to create, process, store, secure and exchange any form of electronic data
- **Management**: organization, planning, coordination and controlling of the activities of a business in order to achieve defined objectives
- **IT Management**: discipline where all the information technology resources of a firm are managed in accordance with its needs and priorities (Source: Wikipedia, the free encyclopedia)

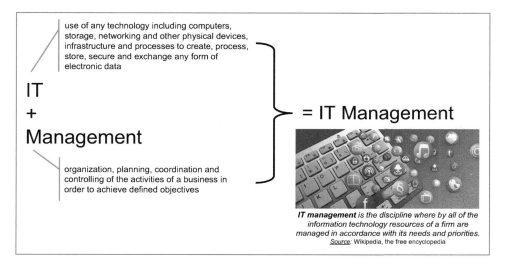

Fig. 1.2 Definition of IT management

IT management should be understood as a holistic way of collecting, processing and storing business data to serve the needs of a company.

It is also interesting to dare a glimpse into the most famous management theories, beginning with Taylorism, as applied by Henry Ford, and ending the list with disruptive innovations as introduced by C. Christensen.

List of Some Major Management Theories

(a) Scientific Management, Frederick Winslow Taylor (1911)
Taylorism is a production methodology that breaks every manufacturing step into small and easily taught tasks in order to improve factory productivity.

(b) Maslow's Hierarchy of Needs, Abraham Maslow (1943)
Maslow's hierachy of needs is a motivational theory represented as a pyramid with the more basic needs at the bottom and self-actualization at the top.

(c) Management by Objectives "MbO", Peter Ferdinand Drucker (1954)
MbO is a performance management technique where challenging but attainable objectives are defined between employees and managers.

(d) Theory X and Theory Y, Douglas McGregor (1960)
Theory X and Theory Y are management theories about human motivation. Theory X is based on pessimistic assumptions of workforce and stresses the importance of strict supervision and penalties whereas in Theory Y managers assume that employees are motivated and look for job satisfaction without direct supervision.

(e) Forming–Storming–Norming–Performing Model of Group Development, Bruce Tuckman (1965)
The model describes the recognizable stages when teams shift from a collection of individuals to a united group with common goals.

(f) PEST "Political, Economic, Sociological, Technological" analysis, Francis J. Aguilar (1967)
The PEST is an analysis tool to scan business environmental elements and get a "big picture".

(g) SWOT (strengths, weaknesses, opportunities, and threats) Analysis, Harvard Business School (1960s)
The SWOT analysis is a framework for identifying and analysing the internal and external factors to find strengths and weaknesses, opportunities and threats to be faced.

(h) BCG Matrix "Cash Cows, Stars, Dogs, Question Marks" (1970s)
The BCG matrix is a concept developed by the Boston Consulting Group that evaluates strategic business units in terms of business growth rate and market shares.

(i) McKinsey 7-S-Model, Robert H. Waterman and Tom Peters (1980s)
The model defines seven key elements (Strategy, Structure, Systems, Staff, Style, Skills, and Superordinate goals) which need to be aligned to improve the performance of an organization.

(j) Porter Five Forces Analysis, Michael E. Porter (1980)
The Porter Five Forces Analysis is a framework for analysing the level of competition within an Industry (bargaining power of suppliers, bargaining power of buyers, threat of new entrants, threat of substitutes, industry rivalry).

(k) SMART „Specific Measurable Accepted Realistic Time Bound" goals, George T. Doran (1981)
The SMART method gives criteria to set objectives.

(l) Change Equation "Dissatisfaction × Vision × First steps > Resistance (D × V × F > R)", Kathie Dannemiller (1992)
Three factors must be taken into account to lead an organizational change: dissatisfaction with how things are now (D), vision of what is possible (V) and first concrete steps that can be taken towards the vision (F). A change is possible if D, V, and F multiplied can overcome the resistance (R).

(m) Disruptive Innovation, Clayton M. Christensen (1995)
A disruptive innovation is an innovation that creates a disruption between existing and new markets.

These theories are helpful to understand companies' decisions. Some of these theories will also be used in this book to illustrate certain aspects of IT management.

1.2   The Meaning of IT

The underlying question is to understand why it is crucial to comprehend IT management in depth. Is it important at all? Is it worth writing a book about it? Well let's have a look at some simple statistics about the importance of IT in our societies.

To start with, let's have a look at the internet revolution. In 2000 the number of internet users was estimated at around 400 million. In the meanwhile, more than three billion people are connected (Source: Statista). This appears to be a dizzying growth rate.

Also the banking industry makes it easy to understand the importance of IT in our world. Transactions between banks are processed by the Society for Worldwide Interbank Financial Telecommunication (SWIFT). In 2016 the average daily SWIFT trade volume represents a processing of more than 25.6 million messages for payments, securities, treasury or trade between 11,299 live users worldwide (Source: SWIFT.com). It is hard to imagine how things could work without IT (Fig. 1.3).

IT is nowadays part of our life from morning to evening. However, as a digital user, everyone has of course many expectations. There is nothing more boring than sitting in front of a computer and waiting for software upgrade installations to be performed. Users expect that IT tools and applications are always available and easy to use. Moreover industry standards in IT are more and more demanding. IT systems must be scalable and secure. Operating systems need to be compatible. An IT manager is not in

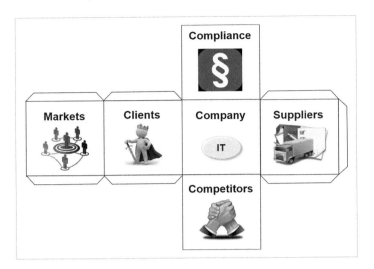

Fig. 1.3 Role of IT in the business game cube

a comfortable situation since different business needs and exacting individual expectations have to be met.

Indeed, the user of a computer sees only "the surface" of the computer environment. Behind the scenes, processes, algorithms, protocols and communication need to be ruled, agreed on, governed, and managed. And not only the technical layers are meant here. IT management has to deal with even more.

Hence, IT management is a determining factor to solve the permanent economic challenges in applying new technologies, developing organisations and optimising business processes (Fig. 1.4)

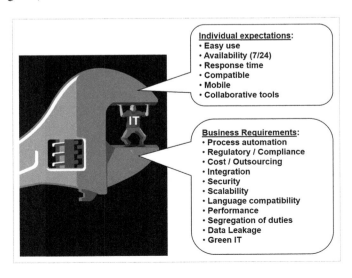

Fig. 1.4 IT under pressure

Questions
1. Is IT a commodity?
2. What are the differences between an IT provider and an electricity supplier? Which are the similarities?
3. Which trends can be perceived in the IT area?

1.3   Organizing the IT

Due to the importance of IT for running the business, most companies have a dedicated IT organisation in place. This organisational structure is in charge of *"running"* and *"changing"* the company, especially by:

- defining necessary policies and procedures
- managing IT assets and the resources needed
- maintaining and operating IT systems (infrastructure and applications)
- supporting IT users
- running IT projects for the continuous improvement of the IT landscape towards usability and innovation

Depending on the size and the culture of the company, the IT may be managed centrally or in a decentral way. A decentralised approach means that each business unit has its own IT department. Even if a centrally managed IT offers many advantages, especially for highly standardised IT services, there is a great temptation for certain business areas to have a "hidden" dedicated IT organisation in place.

The way of organizing the IT itself may vary a lot, depending on the focus and role given to the IT department. Following orientations may be found:

1. Technology driven
   The IT organisation is a collection of technology centric units.
2. Business oriented
   The focus is made on customers with a high process-based orientation.
3. Service oriented
   IT services are shared among the company.
4. IT as a profit centre
   The IT organisation has external customers and is market driven.

Each approach has some benefits and drawbacks, as listed in Table 1.1.

Table 1.1 Pros and cons of IT organisational forms

Organisational form	Advantage	Disadvantage
Technology driven	+ High technical competencies + Economy of scales	− Silo organisation − Low degree of integration between the technical units
Business oriented	+ High dedication and identification with the business + Optimisation of business processes	− High costs − Difficulty to have common standards in place
Service oriented	+ Integration of technical services + Scalability of the services + Charging according to actual use	− Number and relevance of the IT services − Administrative procedures
IT as a profit centre	+ Participate to profit generation + Run IT as a business + Win new markets	− Lesser quality of services − Lack of dedication

The organigram of an IT organization combines most of the time different approaches. For instance, some technical sub-groups (like application development, network administration, datacentre administration or desktop support) are defined whereas transverse dimensions based on shared IT services enable a better business orientation (like business relationship management, service-oriented architecture, provider management or digital services).

At this stage, it is difficult to give general rules to ensure a successful IT organisation as each company has specific needs and particular features. It can be said for sure that the better the integration and acceptance of the IT structure, the higher the chances of managing IT successfully (Fig. 1.5)

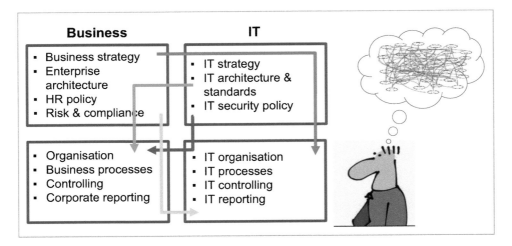

Fig. 1.5 Integrating the IT organisation in a company

Basically, IT management deals with the delivery of IT services required to make sure that the complex digital ecosystem works properly. So IT is often in a sandwich position, trying to balance the company needs with an external delivery of IT services and devices. The interfaces between business and IT and the different governance procedures in place are part of the IT operating model. Decision points, standardised processes, clear and accepted governance, defined roles and responsibilities are typical implementation elements of such an integration framework (Fig. 1.6).

A major difficulty when dealing with IT is for sure the nature and variety of the protagonists. IT in a company setting has many stakeholders involved. Obviously, the management of the company is a key stakeholder to give directions and approve IT investments. IT users build also an essential party of interest. If a system has no user acceptance, then it will be difficult to have efficient processes in place. Compliance officers play inexorably an important role as well (Fig. 1.7).

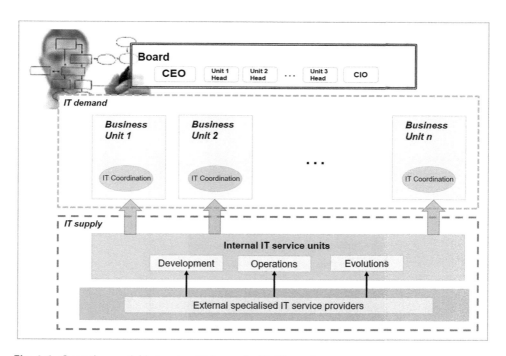

Fig. 1.6 Operating model balancing IT demand with IT supply

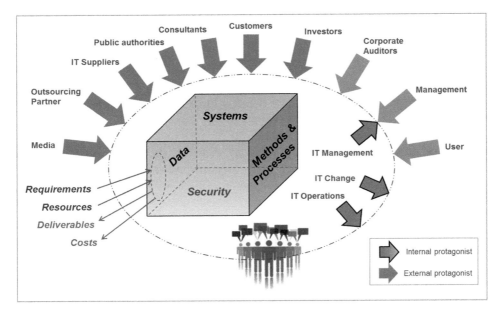

Fig. 1.7 Nature and variety of IT protagonists

The 12 IT Commandments
1. Know the environment
2. Align IT with the company's objectives
3. Manage your vendors
4. Lead the IT organisation
5. Never loose data
6. Be compliant
7. Be prepared for the worst
8. Put standards in place
9. Bring and deliver value
10. Be visible (in a positive way)
11. Enhance technologies
12. Leverage the investment portfolio

External players may sometimes have a great influence. When carrying out a reorganisation, strategy consultants may have every latitude to analyse IT costs and give their recommendations to the senior management. Or if an IT system is directly used by the customers of the company (for instance a sales portal or e-banking), "the voice of the customer"[1] matters a lot.

---

[1] "The voice of the customer" is a term borrowed from the Six Sigma methodology.

Within the IT organisation, the Head IT, the so-called Chief Information Officer (CIO), has a significant influence on the development of the IT business. The CIO is, so to say, the conductor in charge of performing the IT symphony to assure a sustainable development of the IT organisation (Fig. 1.8).

Questions
1. Does the CIO report to the CFO?
2. Is the CIO part of the management board?
3. How is IT perceived in your company?
4. How is IT organised (central or decentral)?

If a company sells IT services, the situation is slightly different as IT customers are "real" customers and not internal customers. The development of the company as a whole is then governed by the laws of the market. New products or product extensions within releases or new services are continuously proposed to existing or new customers. On the buyer side, implementing a new IT solution must meet the needs of the company and has to be planned within the investment cycle (Fig. 1.9).

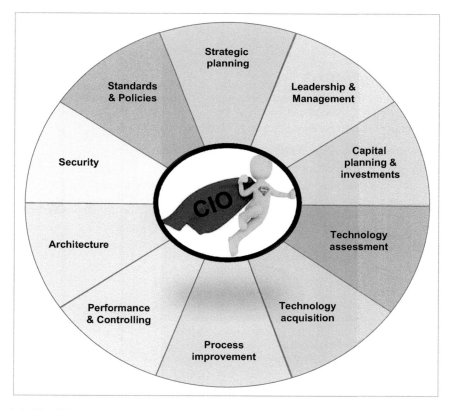

Fig. 1.8 The CIO as superhero

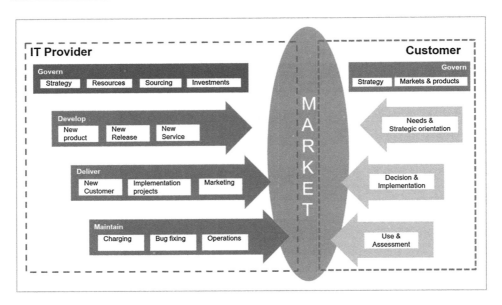

Fig. 1.9 Market model for IT providers

1.4   Sourcing Matters

The sourcing strategy depends on "make-or-buy" decisions. Companies will look for the best IT solutions with maximum efficiency. Three options are possible:

- Deliver the services required internally ("**make**" option),
- Buy the services ("**buy**" option),
- Outsource the corresponding functions or processes ("**outsourcing**" option).

Different criteria are used to take such a decision. In general, the decision will depend on the strategic importance of the area to be outsourced and the availability of external providers (Fig. 1.10).

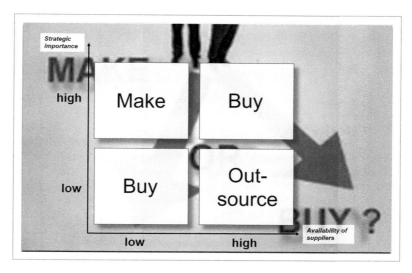

Fig. 1.10 Make or buy? That is the question!

In many cases, a company will set up a map of competencies needed to run the business. This approach enables to assess the best way "to get things done", especially focusing on the identification of critical knowledge.

With the option "make", meaning the service has to be provided internally, the company has to recruit the staff required. On the long term, highly-productive employees must be retained and when introducing new technologies, software specialists must be retrained.

By choosing the option "buy", the company can concentrate on core business. IT is perceived as an interchangeable service and is not necessarily considered to be a strategic component of the business. In such case, business needs can be covered by standard software and applications, perhaps including some minor customisation efforts. In accordance with the "buy" assumption, it is not necessary to recruit specialised IT personnel. The downside is probably the fact that the business cannot expect innovative proposals or impulses from the IT organisation in order to create a competitive advantage.

Undoubtedly it is tempting to consider outsourcing, when assuming that a business can run easier and cheaper with an external IT provider. The wage rate in India is for sure only some per cents of the rate in industrialised countries. Nevertheless, in the longer run, experience shows that outsourcing may lead to an increase of IT spending.

In certain cases, entire business processes are outsourced, which leads to a Business Process Outsourcing (BPO). This practice is not specific to IT as accounting or recruitment for example can also be outsourced.

Here is the definition given by Wikipedia:

*Business process outsourcing is a subset of outsourcing that involves the contracting of the operations and responsibilities of a specific business process to a third-party service provider. Originally, this was associated with manufacturing firms, such as Coca Cola that outsourced large segments of its supply chain. BPO is typically categorized into **back office outsourcing**, which includes internal business functions such as human resources or finance and accounting, and **front office outsourcing**, which includes customer-related services such as contact centre services. BPO that is contracted outside a company's country is called **offshore outsourcing**. BPO that is contracted to a company's neighbouring (or nearby) country is called nearshore outsourcing* (Source: Wikipedia).

When outsourcing is chosen as an option, the relationship between the customer and the outsourcer must be carefully and actively managed. For instance, the outsourcer may capitalise on the IT skills transferred and sell the corresponding competencies to other clients. It may be then challenging to attract and train new talents to maintain and develop existing IT systems at a good quality level.

The decision of outsourcing services depends largely on the experiences gathered by the company. If a first trial was not successful, then of course the management will be reluctant to try a second time.

In the Swiss financial industry, the outsourcing practice is highly regulated and monitored by the federal finance authority FINMA (Swiss Financial Market Supervisory Authority). It is useful to keep the principles defined by FINMA in mind to avoid complications, when turning to the apparent simplicity of outsourcing.

> **Requirements according to FINMA-RS 08/7 „Outsourcing Banks"**
> *Principle 1*: Definition of the outsourcing scope (what has been outsourced?)
> *Principle 2*: Careful selection, instruction and monitoring of the outsourcing partner
> *Principle 3*: Responsibility (the bank remains responsible and accountable)
> *Principle 4*: Security (security issues are properly addressed)
> *Principle 5*: Bank secrecy and data protection (confidentiality according to Swiss law)
> *Principle 6*: Client orientation (clients need to be informed and aware of the outsourcing)
> *Principle 7*: Control and supervision (internal and external auditors need to be informed about all activities)
> *Principle 8*: Farming out in a foreign country (special conditions need to be fulfilled)
> *Principle 9*: Contract (written contract with clear conditions for validity needed)

IT outsourcing includes clearly advantages (+) but also remains a risky undertaking (–):

+ Reduction of costs, especially in terms of investments or recruitment
+ Focus on core business
+ Better quality of services
+ Skilled expertise in specific fields
+ Risk-sharing
− Linguistic and cultural barriers
− Dependencies and loss of managerial control
− Risks concerning security and confidentially
− Hidden costs (low productivity)
− Additional costs when changes occur

Questions

1. Which are the core IT competencies in your company?
2. When is "buy" a good decision?
3. What are the advantages and disadvantages of outsourcing?
4. Which experience made your company in terms of BPO (Business Process Outsourcing)?

Literature

Aguilar FJ (1967) Scanning the business environment. McMillan, London

Christensen CM (1995) Disruptive technologies catching the wave. Harvard Business Review, Cambrigde (MA)

Dannemiller K, Jacobs RW (1992) Changing the way organizations change: a revolution in common sense. J Appl Behav Sci 28:480

Doran GT (1981) There's a S.M.A.R.T. way to write management's goals and objectives. Manag Rev 70:35–36

Drucker P (1954) The practice of management. Harper, New York. Heinemann, London, 1955; revised edn., Butterworth-Heinemann, 2007

Maslow A (1943) Hierarchy of needs: a theory of human motivation. Psychol Rev 50:370–396

McGregor D (1960) Theory X and theory Y printed in "The human side of enterprise". McGraw-Hill, New York 2006

Waterman R Jr, Peters T, Phillips JR (1980) Structure is not organization. Bus Horizons 23, 3 June 1980

Taylor FW (1911) The principles of scientific management. Harper & Brothers, New York 1947

Tuckman BW (1965) Developmental sequence in small groups. Psychol Bull 63:384–399

IT Processes

2

Abstract

Process management enables cost effectiveness and provides the critical added value in the long run. Having proper processes in place is more than just documenting operations: it helps in gaining a deep understanding of the corresponding workflows. Process management also reflects the working spirit, especially the desire to deliver excellent services and the eagerness to continuously improve.

Process management is also a key element to manage IT. In order to implement process management for IT, it is recommended better to define first an overall IT process landscape. Then, it is recommended to re-use existing procedures and in a further step to complete with existing IT process standards. Finally it is necessary to work hard and jointly at the company level to have the IT process management successfully in place.

Several process modelling representations are given in this book and some examples of IT processes are presented.

The implementation and improvement of processes are classical management tasks. It can be said that processes constitute the central nervous system of any organisation. In other words: show me your processes and the way you manage them, and I will tell you how performant your organisation is.

A common understanding of processes is important within an organization in order to enforce a better communication. Time and energy have to be spent to attain the process maturity expected. This also applies to IT processes which need to be managed just the way business processes are.

Modelling interfaced processes presents a major challenge. While modelling one single process is rather easy, it requires much more focussing to design several ones in a consistent manner. Questions might emerge as: Where and when does a process start? When does it end? What are the dependencies to other processes? What is the level of description suitable? What are the concrete steps and their corresponding deliverables?

The key question however remains which processes are needed within an IT organisation at all. In order to answer this question, it is helpful to refer to established process standards and modelling methods, which will provide many insights about the roles needed, the activities related and the interdependencies between processes. Process modelling constitutes the foundation upon which the home of IT will be built.

The current section aims at:

- modelling processes with SIPOC, RACI, Cycle, Flowchart or Swim lane
- knowing IT process standards (ITIL®, COBIT®, IT4IT)
- defining an IT process landscape within three levels (strategic, tactical, operational)
- modelling selected IT processes

2.1   Modelling Processes

Many approaches exist to design and model processes. The range varies from very sophisticated ones, based on BPMN (Business Process Model and Notation) as a standard graphical notation, to basic charts on a paper board. Five different ways of visualizing processes will be presented in this chapter.

> **Questions**
> 1. How are processes modelled in your company?
> 2. Are IT processes included in the design of corporate processes?
> 3. What are the main difficulties about the modelling of processes?

A very useful practice is a Six Sigma diagram, called **SIPOC** (Supplier-Input-Process-Output-Customer) that lists the process steps with the inputs and outputs in a table form (Fig. 2.1).

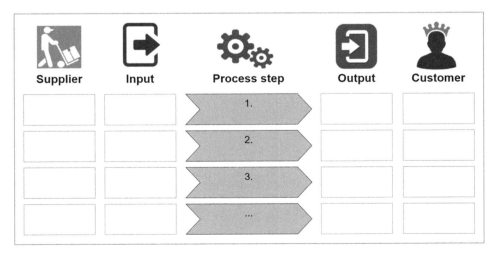

Fig. 2.1 Process modelling with SIPOC (Supplier-Input-Process-Output-Customer)

Give a SIPOC process description to get a cup of coffee:

- Step 1
- Step 2
- …

The Table 2.1 below shows a process description in order to get a cup of coffee from a coffee machine.

You may have designed the process in a different way. This applies especially on the aspect that you may want to select your coffee first and then take an adequate cup.

The **RACI** (Responsible, Accountable, Consulted and Informed) matrix is used in the phase "Improve" of the Six Sigma approach and gives a clear description of the various roles needed when processing business tasks.

RACI makes sure that each task is related to a role and allows a proper assignment within the organisation (Fig. 2.2).

A RACI diagram about "repairing a car" is shown below in Table 2.2.

Table 2.1 Getting a cup of coffee with SIPOC

Supplier	Input	Process	Output	Customer
Catering organisation	Cup from storage	Take a cup	Cup in place	Coffee drinker
Coffee machine manufacturer	Buttons	Check products	Coffee selection	Coffee drinker
Coffee drinker	Selected coffee	Press button	Selected product	Coffee drinker
Coffee supplier	Water, coffee	Prepare coffee	Cup of coffee	Coffee drinker
Catering organisation	Sugar, milk	Add sugar and milk	Cup of coffee ready	Coffee drinker

Example of a SIPOC process description

RACI Matrix
Process Name: ....
Process Owner: ....

Nr.	Process step	Department / Area / Role					Inputs	Outputs	Comments
		A	B	C	D	E			
1									
2									
3									
4									
…									

R: Responsible ("doer" who performs the task and ensures that everything has been completed)
A: Accountable (person in charge, no delegation possible to another role)
C: Consulted (person who gives advice before or during a task completion, can influence a decision)
I: Informed (people or roles informed after finalisation of the task)

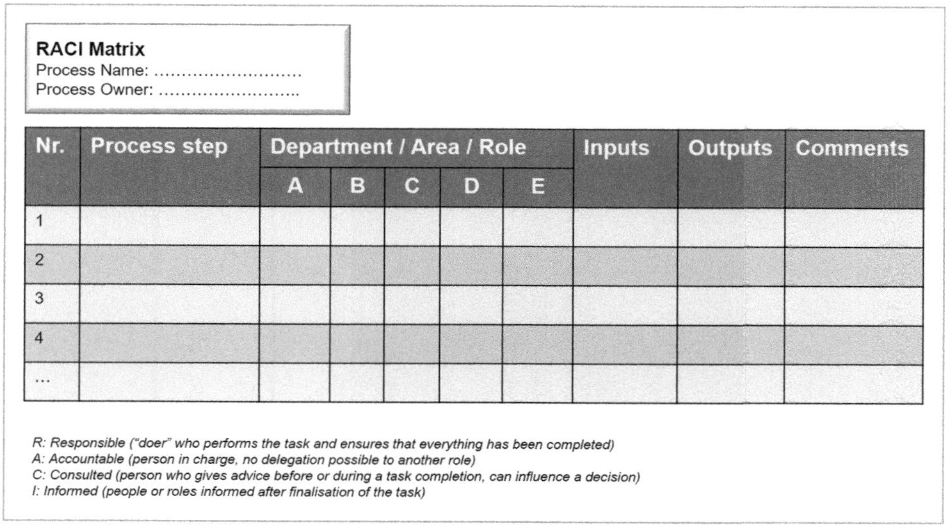

Fig. 2.2 RACI matrix

Table 2.2 RACI diagram "repairing a car"

No	Process step	Person Account Manager	Foreman	Car mechanic	Warehouseman	Director	Inputs	Outputs	Comments
1	Define an appointment with the customer	R				A	Call from customer	Appointment	Ask for car rent
2	Investigate crashed car		R	I	I	A	Car examination	Cost estimate	Check with insurance
3	Procure spare parts		A		R		List of spare parts	Order	Check delay for delivery
4	Repair car	I	A	R			delivered spare parts	repaired car	Inform customer
5	Invoicing reparation	R	C			A	{Time & Material} +10%	Invoice	Check if customer is satisfied

R: Responsible/A: Accountable/C: Consulted/I: Informed

Further ways of representing processes are for instance **flow charts**. A flowchart is a diagram that represents a workflow step-by-step. It visualises a logical sequence of work steps with a formalised structure by using simple geometric symbols and arrows.

When defining such a process from scratch, tasks will be listed first and then assigned to specific roles. After some discussions, it may be necessary to define business rules where some tasks can be only be performed with the input or decision of a stakeholder on the basis of valid competency allocation.

A business process however also often defines a set of activities within an agreed set of sequences and thus follows a formal **life cycle**. This applies especially to recurrent process activities as it is the case in continuous improvement phases.

Questions

1. Which IT processes do you know? Precise the starting trigger and the end.
2. What are typical circular IT processes restarted regularly or even immediately after the former process run is done?
3. Do you know interfaces between processes, where one task of a process triggers another process?

Whereas flow charts are useful when business rules need to be taken into account, cycle representations are often used for recurring lifecycle based activities, similar to some kind of Sisyphus's tasks. Please note that both representations are very similar from a geometric point of view once you can roll a flow chart into a cylinder (Fig. 2.3).

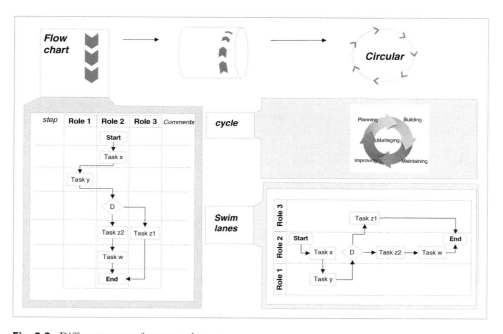

Fig. 2.3 Different ways of representing processes

Swim lane diagrams are also a widespread technique to describe a process from start to finish. The different process steps are identified within lanes indicating which organisational units or roles are relevant for which actions.

The flow chart representation is preferable for a book format, whereas swim lanes are more convenient for "screen oriented" communication.

Exercises

Describe a process of your choice as:

- a flow chart
- a swim lane graph
- a cycle

In addition to an appropriate visualisation, the ten elements shown in Table 2.3 are needed to define, understand and manage a process.

Table 2.3 Process features

Name	Each process should be given an unique name
Description	Short statement to describe the process and its purpose
Objective	Explanation of what has to be accomplished *Objectives should be SMART:* *Specific: What will be accomplished for which target group?* *Measurable: How is the objective quantifiable?* *Achievable: Can the objective be accomplished in the proposed time frame?* *Realistic: Is the objective relevant and in line with overall goals?* *Time-bound: Is a timeline given until when the objective has to be met?*
Trigger	Specific action to be taken by a person, another process, or work group that causes the start of the process
Main steps in a workflow	Series of sequenced or concurrent actions, activities or measures taken to achieve a goal
Output	Result produced by a process step and the overall result of the process
Dependency	Link or relationship between two different processes
Role	Expected behaviour, rights and obligations associated with a particular activity or position
KPI	A **Key Performance Indicator** is a value measured to assess the performance of an organisation (see also Sect. 6.3)
CSF	A **Critical success factor** is an element that is necessary to achieve the process objectives

Ten elements to define, understand and manage a process

List the ten elements needed to define a process for the three following processes:

- IT quality management[1]
- IT service management[2]
- IT supplier management

2.2   Standard IT Processes

Having a clear view of what to achieve with the respective processes is helpful when starting defining IT processes. It is recommended to follow the flowing approach in four steps (Fig. 2.4):

- Be aware of the existing standards (three of them will be presented in the following paragraph)
- Know the existing processes in the organisation and re-use them
- Define the big picture and design the IT process landscape
- Work hard on your processes

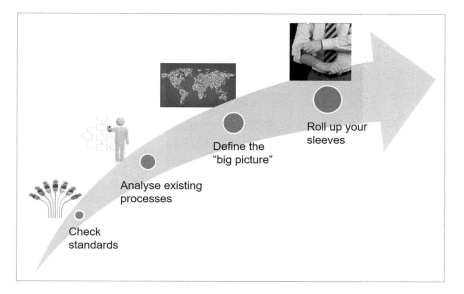

Fig. 2.4 Designing IT processes in 4 steps

---

[1] Quality management deals with the definition of quality standards, rules, and processes in an organization. A public and well known standard for quality management is ISO 9001.

[2] Service Management helps to define clear services for the customer, defines the required processes, infrastructure elements, and resources needed to manage and operate the services. A standard used in IT Service Management is ISO 20000.

Instead of beginning from scratch, the use of existing standards can ease the task of defining IT processes. Three common standards are generally used: ITIL®, COBIT® and IT4IT.

1. Why is the investment into well implemented processes important?
2. What is the probable result of processes with weak definitions or errors?

2.2.1 ITIL® (IT Infrastructure Library)

ITIL® is a standard for IT service management (ITSM) which focuses on aligning IT services with the business needs. Within the ITIL® framework, processes, procedures, tasks and checklists are available and can be applied by any organisation (Fig. 2.5).

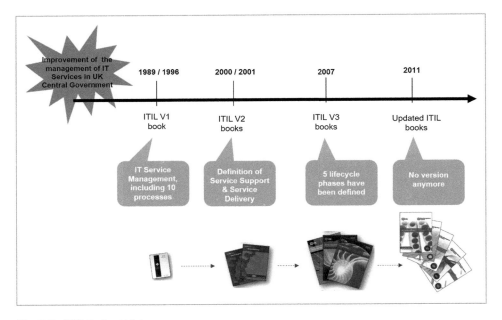

Fig. 2.5 ITIL® short history

Below a list of the topics defined within the ITIL® framework.

List of Topics

Service Strategy: Key Questions for Service Providers

- What IT services should we provide?
- Who should we provide these services to?
- How do we genuinely differentiate from competitors?
- How do we create lasting business value for our customers?
- How can we make a case for ROI and other investments?
- How should we best define and measure service quality?
- How do we choose between different paths for improving service quality?
- How do we efficiently (re)allocate resources across a portfolio of services?
- How do we resolve conflicting demands for shared resources?

Service Design: Processes Included

- Design coordination
- Service catalogue management
- Service level management
- Availability management
- Capacity management
- IT service continuity management
- Information security management
- Supplier management

Service Transition: Processes Included

- Knowledge management
- Transition planning and support
- Change management
- Availability management
- Service asset and configuration management (SACM)
- Release and deployment management
- Evaluation

Service Operation: Four Main Functions

- Technical management
  - Manage the IT infrastructure
  - Provide skilled staff and support operations staff members
- Application management
  - Manage the IT applications
  - Ensure knowledge and provide training to technical staff

- Operations management
  - Conduct day-to-day activities to ensure that SLA (Service Level Agreement) is met
  - Ensure availability and stability of IT systems
  - Schedule and monitor batch-jobs
- Service desk
  - SPOC (Single Point of Contact) for users of IT services
  - Prioritise issues and escalates if necessary
  - Solves as far as possible incidents

Continual Service Improvement (CSI) in Seven Steps

1. Identify the strategy for improvement
2. Define what you will measure
3. Gather the data
4. Process the data
5. Analyse the information and data
6. Present and use the information
7. Implement improvement

Applying ITIL® presents many advantages:

- Reduced costs for the organisation
- Better productivity of the organisation
- Improved IT services through the use of proven best practice processes
- Improved quality control
- Improved use of skills and experience of the employees
- Improved customer satisfaction
- Use of industry standards
- Improved delivery of third party services if ITIL® is used as a common standard between the service recipient and the service provider

Nevertheless, the following points must be also taken into account, when considering ITIL® as a standard for IT processes:

- Extensive use may lead to considerable costs
- Not easily comprehensible, since ITIL® is already in its fourth iteration
- Training and certification required

2.2.2   COBIT® (Control Objectives for Information and Related Technology)

COBIT® is a framework for IT governance and management practices created by ISACA (Information Systems Audit and Control Association). ISACA released the first COBIT® version in 1996. The current version, COBIT® 5, was published in 2012. According to

ISACA, *"COBIT® 5 helps enterprises create optimal value from IT by maintaining a balance between realizing benefits, optimizing risk levels and resource use. It enables information and related technology to be governed and managed in a holistic manner, considering the related interests of internal and external stakeholders."* It consists of a process governance model, a series of governance and management practices and a set of enabler tools.

COBIT® 5 particularly specifies five principles and seven main enablers. It also gives useful guidance for the implementation of IT processes and governance.

The five principles of COBIT® 5 are (Fig. 2.6):

1. **Meeting Stakeholder Needs**
   The aim is to create value for the organisation and ultimately for the customers
2. **Covering the Enterprise End-to-End**
   Roles, activities and relationships between the different protagonists among the complete value creation chain are clear
3. **Single Integrated Framework**
   COBIT® 5 is aligned with other standards and is foreseen as an integrative framework
4. **Enabling a Holistic Approach**
   COBIT® 5 takes individual and collective factors into account to understand the different influences and to steer the organisation to the achievement of its goals
5. **Separating Governance from Management**
   Governance embraces evaluation, decision-making and monitoring activities (Evaluate, Direct and Monitor) whereas management is in charge of planning, building, running and monitoring

Fig. 2.6 COBIT® 5 5 principles (Source: COBIT® 5, figure 2. © 2012 ISACA®)

The seven COBIT® 5 enablers are:

1. **Principles, Policies and Frameworks**
   Emphasised practical guidance for day-to-day management to straighten expected behaviour across the organisation
2. **Processes**
   Series of tasks and activities organised in a standardised manner to achieve enterprise goals
3. **Organisational Structures**
   Management and coordination of resources to enable decision making and delivery of products or services
4. **Culture, Ethics and Behaviour**
   Elements that influence morale, productivity and an organisation's reputation
5. **Information**
   Key asset for the effective and efficient management of a company, including either produced or used information
6. **Services, Infrastructure and Applications**
   Sum of infrastructure, technologies and IT tools needed to process the company activities
7. **People, Skills and Competencies**
   Main asset of a company as human capital required to produce products or services

Enablers are interconnected. For instance, processes will generate new information or skills, which are needed to use applications (Fig. 2.7).

COBIT® 5 contains also 37 process references.

---

37 Processes for Management of Enterprise IT within the COBIT® 5 Process Reference Model

Evaluate, Direct and Monitor

- EDM 01; Ensure Governance Framework Setting and Maintenance
- EDM 02, Ensure Benefits Delivery
- EDM 03, Ensure Risk Optimisation
- EDM 04, Ensure Resource Optimisation
- EDM 05, Ensure Stakeholder Transparency

Align, Plan and Organise

- APO 01, Manage the IT Management Framework
- APO 02, Manage Strategy
- APO 03, Manage Enterprise Architecture

- APO 04, Manage Innovation
- APO 05, Manage Portfolio
- APO 06, Manage Budget and Costs
- APO 07, Manage Human Resources
- APO 08, Manage Relationships
- APO 09, Manage Service Agreements
- APO 10, Manage Suppliers
- APO 11, Manage Quality
- APO 12, Manage Risk
- APO 13, Manage Security

Build, Acquire and Implement

- BAI 01, Manage Programmes and Projects
- BAI 02, Manage Requirements Definition
- BAI 03, Manage Solutions Identification and Build
- BAI 04, Manage Availability and Capacity
- BAI 05, Manage Organisational Change Enablement
- BAI 06, Manage Changes
- BAI 07, Manage Change Acceptance and Transitioning
- BAI 08, Manage Knowledge
- BAI 09, Manage Assets
- BAI 10, Manage Configuration

Deliver, Service and Support

- DSS 01, Manage Operations
- DSS 02, Manage Service Requests and Incidents
- DSS 03, Manage Problems
- DSS 04, Manage Continuity
- DSS 05, Manage Security Services
- DSS 06, Manage Business Process Controls

Monitor, Evaluate and Assess

- MEA 01, Monitor, Evaluate and Assess Performance and Conformance
- MEA 02, Monitor, Evaluate and Assess the System of Internal Control
- MEA 03, Monitor, Evaluate and Assess Compliance with External Requirements

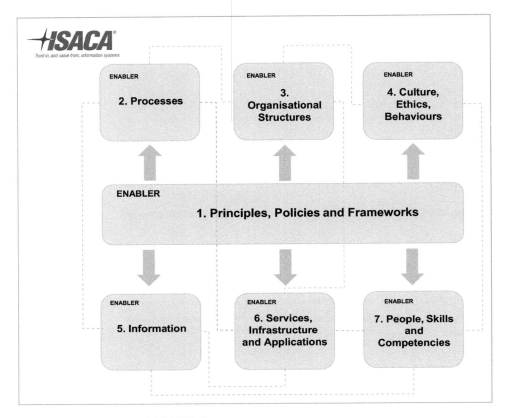

Fig. 2.7   Seven enablers of COBIT® 5

COBIT® 5 offers an IT framework, which helps companies to realise their benefits by optimising their IT investments, minimising theirs risks and making an optimal usage of their resources.

While ITIL® is introduced and used by IT organizations in the field of IT operations for tactical and operational purposes, COBIT® is often used by the upper IT management to steer IT from a strategic and tactical point of view. In order to solve the dilemma of having two standards concurrently used, literature is provided by the delivering editors, ICASA and the OGC, with a mapping of processes and terminology.

2.2.3   IT4IT (Open Group)

The **Open Group** is a software standards organization founded in 1996 with more than 500 members and acts as a vendor- and technology-neutral industry consortium (see http://www.opengroup.org).

The Open Group publishes a reference architecture for managing the business of IT, called **IT4IT**. It stipulates that the IT4IT model is largely inspired from manufacturing practices like value chain and lean manufacturing. It includes four main steps to describe the value chain integration:

Strategy to Portfolio (S2P)

- Strategy
- Service Portfolio
- Demand
- Selection

Requirement to Deploy (R2D)

- Plan & Design
- Develop
- Test
- Deploy

Request to Fulfil (R2F)

- Define & Publish
- Subscribe
- Fulfil
- Measure

Detect to Correct (D2C)

- Detect
- Diagnose
- Change
- Resolve

The model is completed with five so-called support activities (see Fig. 2.8 below):

- Finance & Assets
- Sourcing & Vendor
- Intelligence & Reporting
- Resource & Project
- Governance, Risk and Compliance

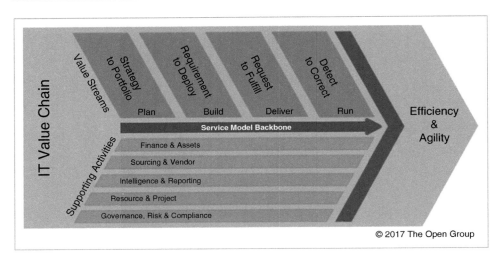

Fig. 2.8 IT4IT Value chain

Within IT4IT an IT reference architecture has also been defined, including the following components:

1. **Strategy to Portfolio**
   - Enterprise Architecture Functional Component
   - Policy Functional Component
   - Proposal Functional Component
   - Portfolio Demand Functional Component
   - Service Portfolio Functional Component
   - IT Investment Portfolio Auxiliary Functional Component
2. **Requirement to Deploy**
   - Project Functional Component
   - Requirement Functional Component
   - Service Design Functional Component
   - Source Control Functional Component
   - Build Functional Component
   - Build Package Functional Component
   - Release Composition Functional Component
   - Test Functional Component
   - Defect Functional Component
3. **Request to Fulfil**
   - Engagement Experience Portal (Secondary Functional Component)
   - Offer Consumption Functional Component
   - Offer Management Functional Component

- Catalogue Composition Functional Component
- Request Rationalisation Functional Component
- Fulfilment Execution Functional Component
- Usage Functional Component
- Chargeback/Show back Functional Component
- Knowledge & Collaboration Supporting Function

4. **Detect to Correct**
- Service Monitoring Functional Component
- Event Functional Component
- Incident Functional Component
- Problem Functional Component
- Change Control Functional Component
- Configuration Management Functional Component
- Diagnostics & Remediation Functional Component
- Service Level Functional Component
- Other IT Operations Areas

The advantage of the IT4IT model is its integrative end-to-end approach to manage the business of IT. Especially the relationships between the different components are clearly identified. IT4IT offers an answer to manage an increasingly complex IT estate in a more cost-effective way. It proposes a *"value chain-based operating model"* which is complementary to existing standards like ITIL® or COBIT®.

2.3   IT Process Landscape

Defining and documenting processes is a complex task, and it does not always bring the expected results right at the first attempt. Nevertheless, two major advantages are achieved when designing processes:

1. A common understanding of the IT business is gained
2. A company-wide language regarding IT glossary, roles, processes and technical elements is in place

Experience shows also that the process of getting IT processes in place is even more important than the documentation of the processes itself. In this regard, it is essential to have a clear idea how to proceed and where to start.

One approach to document IT processes is to begin from scratch, replacing all given processes, roles, and terms used in the organization so far. This approach has the advantage of enabling a new view on all topics and items in the organization but also bears the risk of becoming quite time-consuming and leading to a dead end due to the complexity. There is also the high risk that the new set-up is never accepted during its implementation.

A second idea is to start bottom-up and to consider the existing processes. In this pragmatic approach the difficulty lies in the "reconciliation" between the different processes and the consistency within the interdependencies.

The recommended approach is to define a big picture first. By doing this, a process scope is defined in advance and within this given perimeter the activities for designing and documenting the processes can be coordinated. In that way, a process landscape is first defined and the documentation of the processes identified can start.

Three elements are helpful to get a consistent IT process landscape (Fig. 2.9):

- **IT customers**
  Depending on which management level needs to be involved, it is possible to categorise the processes into a) relevant for the upper management b) relevant for the middle management and c) relevant for IT users.
- **Time frame**
  Some processes need to be conducted within minutes (helpdesk activities) whereas others run once a year (budgeting for instance). It is possible to distinguish strategic processes (timescale = year), tactical processes (timescale = month) and operational processes (time scale = week).
- **IT suppliers**
  Depending on the amount of the investments and the contractor's commitment, it is possible to differentiate between partners, providers and sellers.

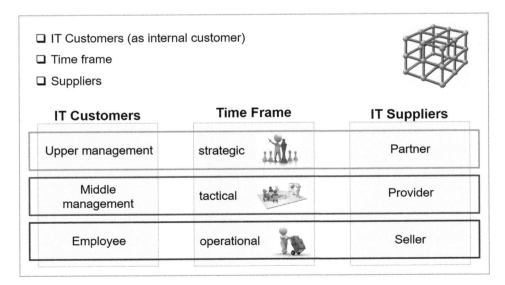

Fig. 2.9 Structuring elements to define the IT process landscape

Following major difficulties may arise when defining an IT process landscape:

- different IT process models are already in place
- no integration into the business process map
- no big picture (each IT department has its specific processes)
- interdependencies between the different IT processes are not defined

After having defined the different layers of a process landscape, it becomes easier to segregate the different processes into "strategic", "tactical" or "operational" layers. It has to be noted that a process may belong to several categories depending on its positioning. In addition, some processes run concurrently on each level, e.g. reporting processes for the various stakeholder groups (Fig. 2.10).

Exercises

Write a list of IT processes defined in your company and indicate whether the processes are of strategic, tactical or operational nature:

- Process 1: .... (strategic/tactical/operational)
- Process 2: .... (strategic/tactical/operational)
- Process 3: .... (strategic/tactical/operational)
- Process 4: .... (strategic/tactical/operational)
- Process 5: .... (strategic/tactical/operational)
- Process 6: .... (strategic/tactical/operational)

In the subsequent chapters, the presentations and results are based on the IT landscape as shown in Fig. 2.11 (see L. Pilorget 2015).

The IT process landscape proposed contains 17 different processes. Availability and capacity are combined in one process. Furthermore, no specific process is defined concerning IT security. The two ideas beyond this are the following:

- Security is included within the process "IT Standards & Architecture" at a strategic level
- Security activities need to be taken into consideration at all levels, for instance within projects or when defining operational activities

The more processes on a landscape, the more precise the framework is. However too many processes will cause difficulty in keeping consistency and in representing all relationships in place. Here again, the key question remains the definition of the need to be met: having a simplified overview which enables a holistic understanding of processes or documenting all processes in a very detailed and specific way.

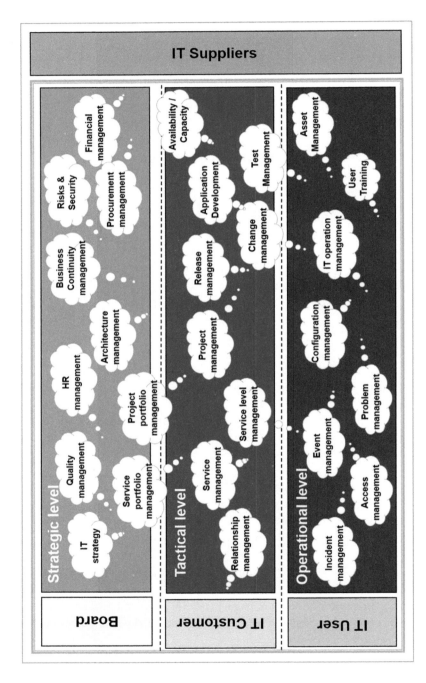

Fig. 2.10 Classification of the IT processes in strategic, tactical and operational layers

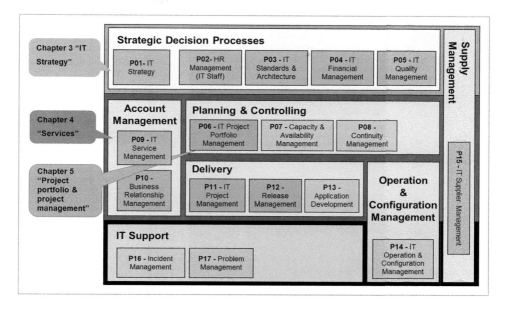

Fig. 2.11 Proposed IT process landscape

2.4   Design of IT Processes

Once having defined an IT process landscape, it is possible to document the different processes identified.

In the following chapter, a description of five selected IT processes will be given using different modelling forms for their representation:

- IT Quality Management => Cycle
- Application Development => Flow
- IT Supplier Management => Swim Lane
- Incident Management => SIPOC
- Problem Management => RACI

2.4.1   IT Quality Management Cycle

The main objective of IT quality management is to ensure that proper quality is delivered. This happens by setting quality standards and measuring the quality delivered within services and projects.

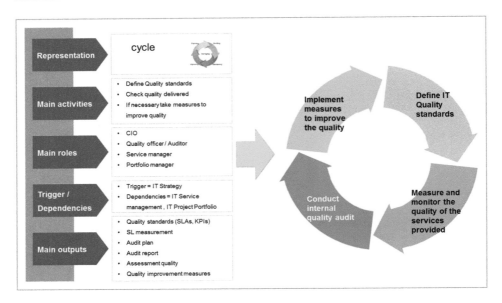

Fig. 2.12 The IT quality management cycle

The main activities within this process can be summarised in four steps, all done in a regular cycle (Fig. 2.12):

1. Define the IT quality standards
2. Measure and monitor the quality of the services provided
3. Conduct internal quality audits
4. Implement measures to improve the quality

The process is triggered by the IT strategy and depends on the processes "service management" and "project portfolio management".

Implementing the process, roles need to be defined as in Table 2.4 and KPIs should be set as in Table 2.5. Critical success factors are:

• Set clear definition of quality criteria and levels
• Agree on measurement procedures
• Share and learn from experience gained
• Understand quality audit as a good opportunity to progress
• Be transparent and honest

Table 2.4 Process roles for the IT quality management process

Role 1: CIO	Establishes the quality standards for the specified IT services
	Initiates appropriate measures in response to detected quality deficiencies
	Ensures compliance with the defined quality standards
	Is accountable for the overall quality compliance
Role 2: Quality officer	Supports the CIO to establish the quality standards
	Is responsible for the organisation and planning of internal audits
	Submits the results of audits to the CIO
	Makes sure that the approved measures are implemented and that the detected quality deficiencies are effectively addressed
Role 3: Head service management	Defines, measures and monitors compliance with the established service levels
Role 4: Project portfolio manager	Defines project KPIs
	Measures project performance
	Organises lessons learned and implements improvement measures

Table 2.5 Process KPIs for IT quality management process

KPIs	Definition	Measurement
KPI 1	Zero Default	Number of violations to standards defined (e.g. according to a Service Level Agreement)
		Project performance based on the measurement of the project KPIs
KPI 2	Audit culture	Number of audits per year
		Audit frequency per IT area
KPI 3	Implementation of quality improvement measures	Number of implemented quality improvements

2.4.2   Application Development Flow

Application development aims at delivering high quality SW solutions. The process starts with business requirements and ends with a quality check, called in general unit and integration tests.

Following steps are needed in order to have the process in place (Table 2.6, Fig. 2.13):

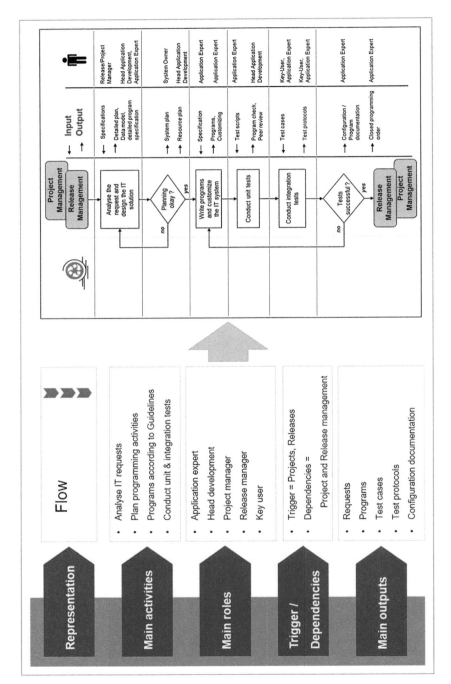

Fig. 2.13 Application development flow

Table 2.6 Process steps for application development

Main step	Description
Analyse requirements	Programme specifications are defined
Draft a development plan	The programming activities are defined and a rough effort estimate can be given
Programme	The programming is done
Check quality of the development	The quality of the programming is done, either by reviewing the code or by testing the programme
Deliver the programme	The programme is delivered to the requester

The proposed description is based on the assumption that the application development process is triggered by the project and release management processes where business specifications are delivered.

In the SW development area, new methods have been developed to accelerate the delivery of programmed solutions. The so-called agile approaches enable rapid cycles of development to avoid situations in which at the end of a long process the requester is confronted with a solution which does not correspond to the real needs of the business. This kind of "Scrum" practice is not included at this stage in the process description.

For this process, roles are listed in Table 2.7 and KPIs in Table 2.8.

Critical success factors are:

- Availability of the developing resources
- Business knowledge and good understanding of the company needs
- Good communication and avoidance of "jumping to solutions" behaviours
- Sustainability of the programmed solutions
- Time-to-delivery

Table 2.7 Process roles for application development

Role 1: Application expert/ Programmer	Reviews the requirements
	Drafts estimations of the associated costs and proposes detailed plans (activities + resource availability)
	Defines logical data models
	Programmes or parameterises and completes product tests
	Provides support when it comes to the execution of integration tests, acceptance tests and training programmes
	Documents programmes and configuration elements
Role 2: Head development	Checks the feasibility of the IT requirements (resource planning, cost estimation)
	Approves specifications
	Checks development quality according to programming guidelines
	Ensures the availability of the relevant documentation

(continued)

Table 2.7   (continued)

Role 3: Project manager	Conveys the relevant orders from the project Coordinates the drafting of the project plan, including the detailed plan for the established development (activities + resources)
Role 4: Release manager	Conveys the relevant orders from the release Coordinates the drafting of the release plan, including the detailed plan for the established development (activities + resources)
Role 5: Key user	Reviews the specifications Carries out integration tests Issues approval for development closure
Role 6: System owner	Reviews current release plans on the basis of system planning Makes the IT infrastructure available

Table 2.8   Process KPIs for application development

KPIs	Definition	Measurement
KPI 1	Functionality fulfilment	Suitability and applicability of the delivered programme, by strict comparison of single functions and by end-user survey
KPI 2	Development costs	Programming effort
KPI 3	Number of bugs per line of code <2.5 per thousand	Number of bugs Re-testing effort
KPI 4	Quality of the programmes Re-usability of the SW solutions	Number of reworks SW repository and delivery time

2.4.3   IT Supplier Management Swim Lane

The IT supplier management process aims at the suitable delivery of external devices or services at a cost-effective market level. It represents a critical process for the whole company where legal, financial, technological as well as business interests need to be taken into account to optimise the value added to the organisation.

Following steps are necessary in order to have the process in place (Table 2.9, Fig. 2.14). The supplier management process is related to the IT operation & configuration process

Table 2.9 Process steps for IT supplier management

Main step	Description
Define purchase requirements	The company has to have clearly defined needs and has to set frames for the selection of suppliers
Select a suitable supplier	The supplier should be a reliable partner, cost-effective and committed to quality. The terms of the service provision are to be specified in a signed agreement The decision on the selection of a supplier has to be taken by the management
Order and take delivery of the goods or services	The goods and services are provided after the purchase order has been submitted All of the various deliverables are checked for completeness and quality in the context of an acceptance procedure
Carry out installation and use products or services	*Operation*: The purchased products are installed and brought into operation *Project*: The supplier's employees are trained and integrated into the project team
Check and pay the invoices	The purchased products and the rendered services are invoiced. The invoices are reviewed, entered into the books and paid
Assess the quality of the supplier	It is important to keep a record of the quality and cost-effectiveness of the provided goods and services. Supplier performance should be systematically evaluated after the goods and services are provided. A short list of IT suppliers should be kept and updated as appropriate

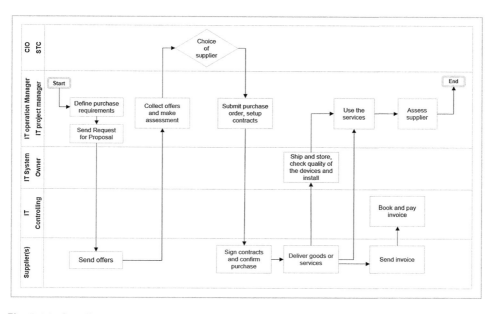

Fig. 2.14 Supplier management swim lane

due to the purchase of IT devices, material and services. It is also dependent on the project management process as it is triggered by project purchase requirements. It also shows an interdependence to the IT financial management process due to charging and invoicing.

The responsibilities of the IT operations and project manager are often delegated to a central corporate supplier manager, whose role is the selection and the management of external suppliers.

Find roles in Table 2.10, KPIs in Table 2.11 and critical success factors below:

- Well understood business needs
- Time and planning to have supplier selection in place
- Transparent procedure for the selection of suppliers
- Management involvement
- Choice of reliable suppliers, not only based on financial considerations
- Open and direct communication

Table 2.10 Process roles for IT supplier management

Role 1: IT operations manager	• Drafts order requirements for purchasing IT devices • Commissions the provision of all of the necessary services and hardware and software products included in the operational budget • Orders all of the hardware and software that is necessary for the given projects in consultation with the project manager • Ensures the compliance of all services and hardware and software products commissioned in the context of operational activities with the applicable IT standards (exceptions are forwarded to the CIO) • Evaluates the performance of all suppliers • Maintains a record of supplier performance and updates the supplier short list whenever appropriate
Role 2: Project manager	• Drafts order requirements for project needs • Commissions all of the approved and budgeted services that are necessary for a successful completion of projects • Makes sure that the services and the hardware and software products that are commissioned in the context of projects correspond to the IT standards • Evaluates the service performance of the suppliers • Maintains a record of supplier performance and updates the supplier short list whenever appropriate
Role 3: CIO	• Takes decision on the choice of suppliers • Agrees to exceptions of standards

(continued)

Table 2.10 (continued)

Role 4: STC	• Takes final decision on the selection of a solution and the corresponding supplier
Role 5: System owner	• Receives the delivered devices • Checks system quality and completeness • Performs preliminary installations and corresponding tests • Installs and commissions delivered equipment
Role 6: IT controlling	• Makes sure that agreements have been drafted and signed before orders are placed or processed • Records external invoices • Is responsible for checking the accuracy of invoices • Forwards reviewed invoices to the accounting office for payment
Role 7: Supplier	• Submits offers upon request • Signs agreements to provide specified products or services • Delivers specified products and provides specified services • Submits an invoice for products and services provided

Table 2.11 Process KPIs for IT supplier management

KPIs	Definition	Measurement
KPI 1	Delivery schedules	Number of complaints caused by a lack of equipment or unavailable services
KPI 2	Market prices	Benchmark analysis Supply chain and reported inventory value
KPI 3	Orders in accordance to defined IT standards	Number of orders outside of the standards
KPI 4	Supplier assessment	Standardised criteria to be fulfilled by each supplier

2.4.4   Incident Management SIPOC

The incident management process is an operational process whose purpose is to ensure the quickest possible restoration of services in the wake of service outages or loss of delivery quality. Service recovery should be achieved by the specified maximum service restoration time.

Process triggers are incoming calls, emails or web messages from users. SIPOC Table 2.12 describes the incident management process in five steps. Two cases can be considered for incident management:

- 1st case: the user's need can be directly addressed by the helpdesk
- 2nd case: the involvement of the second level support is needed

If the incident cannot be solved by the 2nd level support at all, it can be identified as a problem and processed by the problem management process, which will be described in the next paragraph.

Following dependencies need to be taken into account:

- **Problem management**: if the incident cannot be (easily) solved and depending on its priority, a problem has to be raised and the problem management process needs to be activated
- **IT operations**: in certain cases, a system change may be needed. E.g. parts need to be replaced, or a bug needs to be fixed
- **Requirement management**: in some cases, the issue reported by the user has to be addressed by a request to be treated within the requirement management process

Table 2.12   SIPOC table for incident management

Step	S	I	P	O	C
1	User	Call, mail, web-issue	Create a call ticket and enter relevant information	Call ticket	Helpdesk
2	User, Helpdesk	Call analysis	Provide 1st level support and determine ticket priority	Solved call ticket or incident ticket	User in case call solved, helpdesk
3	Helpdesk	Incident ticket	Create an incident ticket and send it to 2nd level support	Assigned incident ticket	2nd level support
4	2nd level support	Processed incident ticket	Resolves the incident, documents the resolution and notifies helpdesk	Solved incident	Helpdesk
5	Helpdesk	Solved incident	Contact user and close incident ticket	User's feedback and closed ticket	User

The process description makes it possible to define the roles needed (Table 2.13). KPIs mentioned in Table 2.14 can be put in place.
Below some of the critical success factors are specified:

- Good information to users how to reach the helpdesk
- Friendly agents to assure the acceptance of the helpdesk services by users
- Good knowledge of the IT organisation to make sure that incident tickets are sent to the proper 2nd level unit
- Tracking of the tickets to avoid "ping-pong" situations
- Enabling helpdesk agents to solve "simple" incidents by themselves, just like "reset password"

Table 2.13   Process roles for incident management

Role 1: User	• Reports usability issue • Approves responses and solutions • Assesses service quality
Role 2: Helpdesk	• Answers phone calls • Documents issue in a call ticket, provides first aid • Sets up incident priorities • Drafts and forwards incident tickets to 2nd level support • Closes out tickets and notifies user
Role 3: 2nd level support	• Receives incident tickets • Analyses and resolves incidents according to ticket priorities • Drafts problem tickets in response to complex incidents • Notifies helpdesk on ticket status

Table 2.14   Process KPIs for incident management

KPIs	Definition	Measurement
KPI 1	Helpdesk reachability	Number of missed calls
KPI 2	Helpdesk efficiency	Index of helpdesk self-resolution
KPI 3	Costs	Price of a call or incident ticket
KPI 4	Knowledge data base about known errors	Number of data entries and "usable" requests

In order to have the process in place, it makes sense to launch a project. Acknowledging the current situation, it is important to assess the needs for helpdesk services and to answer two key questions:

- In which languages should the helpdesk services be provided?
- What should be the helpdesk's availability? E.g. 24 by 7 , implemented as "follow the sun"[3]

Since the incident management process is one of the most often introduced IT processes, it is recommended to select and adapt an already published process model and to implement a professional tool solution. Incident management without a ticketing system is not a very good idea. The project's steering committee should be aware of given solutions and approve an appropriate budget to buy licences.

Having a tool in place means that a suitable organisation for the maintenance of the solution is available and corresponding operational costs are budgeted. An option is to investigate and check if an outsourcing solution may be an alternative.

During a first phase it is necessary to make decisions concerning solution based on a help-desk tool, internally or within an outsourcing, which languages and which reachability.

In a second phase, the concept concerning the proposed solution should be planned in detail. Given the case that a tool solution is put in place (no outsourcing), negotiations with different providers should take place and a contract with the selected supplier should then be signed.

In the building phase, the system will be installed (a test environment needs to be foreseen). Helpdesk agents need to be recruited and trained. A communication to the organisation and the IT users is also necessary. An interface to a CMDB (Configuration Management Data Base) should be foreseen in order to have all the necessary user information available in the helpdesk application.

Having the solution in place, after user acceptance tests have been successfully achieved, a proper structure for the 2nd Level support units is required, also some knowledge data base for known errors, user manuals and process description.

In the final part of the project, a survey should be planned in order to have feedbacks from users. Process KPIs should be defined and measured to make sure that the process is properly managed.

Exercises

Based on helpdesk statistics please list the most frequent incidents encountered by your company:

- Top 1:
- Top 2:
- Top 3:

---

[3]To achieve 24 h availability on 7 days the week, global companies may set-up three or four help-desks in different time zones having the same level of knowledge and privileges. The tickets "follow the sun".

2.4.5   Problem Management RACI

The problem management process deals with solving the underlying cause of incidents or disturbances. The aim is to resolve the root cause of errors and to find permanent solutions. Furthermore the problem management process is used as the major source to collect knowledge on IT solutions and services.

The following approach proves to be very useful to manage problems:

Step 1: Analyse the situation
The purpose of analysing the situation is to arrive at a better understanding of the reported issue and it possible causes within the infrastructure or application:

- Describe the reported issue in an accessible manner
- Obtain any relevant information. Seek for related incident reports from other sources
- Demarcate the problem
- Classify the problem (impact, urgency, priority). What has been reported in an incident?

Step 2: Seek the underlying cause (error)
A reported incident has an underlying root cause which has to be found and either eliminated or circumvented.

- Seek possible root causes
- Investigate if a root can be the "real" cause of the reported symptoms
- Select one of the possible causes and describe
- Try to find a workaround, how the service can be delivered bypassing the cause

Step 3: Document known error
In the moment a root cause is identified as an error within an application or within the infrastructure, it has to be published as such to avoid further incident reports

- Document the underlying cause as a known error ($\rightarrow$ knowledge management)
- Inform service desk and 2nd level user support about its existence
- Communicate the workaround

Step 4: Investigate in possible solutions
Based on economical and efficient thoughts, identify possible solutions for the elimination of the error.

- Is the solution feasible in a specific frame of time and effort?
- Does the provider of the equipment or application delivers a solution (patch, upgrade) in near future?
- If not, can the users live with the workaround for a longer time or even forever?
- Document pros and cons of the solution and display costs and gains

Step 5: Invest in a resolution

If the change authority of the IT organization has decided to implement the solution, the IT architects, developers or service delivery managers start with its implementation.

- Buy or rent additional, new, or more reliable equipment
- Develop, test and roll-out a software update or release
- Update configurations in the settings of existing services
- Inform helpdesk and 2nd level support about the elimination of the error

Step 6: Evaluate the result

The implemented solution is reviewed to determine whether the problem has been resolved or not.

A RACI table is proposed to describe the process (Table 2.15).

Following dependencies need to be taken into account:

- **Incident management**: if the incident cannot be (easily) solved and depending on its priority, a problem ticket is open and the problem management process is activated
- **Release Management**: in case a change needs to be implemented, the release management process will be activated
- **Requirement management**: in specific situations, the problem needs to be addressed by a request to be treated within the requirement management process

Based on the process description, it is possible to identify the roles required (Table 2.16). The problem management process should be used on a case by case basis. Undoubtedly it is possible to define the corresponding KPIs. Nevertheless, the principal interest lays in the organisational responsiveness of IT.

Following KPIs can be put in place (Table 2.17).

Some critical success factors are listed below:

- Awareness of IT management and proper identification of problem areas (performance, availability, …)
- Availability of experts needed within a task force
- Compliance to change procedures
- Permanent and good communication to the users impacted

Table 2.15 RACI table for problem management

No	Process step	IT operations manager	Problem owner	Task force member	System owner	Input	Output	Comments
1	Start problem management process and define the problem area	A, R	I		C	Incident report(s) in a specific service	Nomination of a problem owner	Awareness needed
2	Analyse current symptoms	A	R	I	C	Incidents, user testimonials	As-is analysis	
3	Seek for underlying causes	A	R	R	C	System/service information	Possible root causes	Investigation by experts
4	Select one cause and document as known error		A	R	C	possible causes	Known error/workaround	
5	Inform		A, R			Known error/workaround	Informed helpdesk	Avoid further incident reports
6	Analyse possible resolutions, weight	A	R	R	C	Cost of proposed resolutions	None or one selected solution	
7	Implement the solution		A		R	Change proposal	Change processed	Planning needed
8	Assess resolution	A	I	I	R	Descriptions of error and solution	Solution check	Close problem
9	Inform	A	C		R	solution	Informed helpdesk	Workarounds have to be stopped

Table 2.16 Process roles for problem management

Role 1: IT operations manager	Initiates the problem management process Approves responses and solutions Names the problem owner Is accountable for the solution of the problem
Role 2: Problem owner	Is in charge of conducting the problem management process Conducts the task force for the analysis of the problem Analyses root causes and identifies underlying error Investigates in corrective measures Makes sure that the implementation of the solution is done correctly
Role 3: Task force member	Completes the assignments given by the problem owner Reports progress on activities planned
Role 4: System owner	Implements system changes according to the procedures in place Monitors system performance Ensures quality of the running system

Table 2.17 Process KPIs for problem management

KPIs	Definition	Measurement
KPI 1	Stability of service/system	Number of incidents before and after problem has been resolved
KPI 2	Effectiveness of problem management	Average time between problem reported and investigation completed

Literature

Pilorget L (2015) Implementing IT processes. Springer, Wiesbaden

IT Strategy

3

Abstract

Strategy is a formidable discipline where the business areas of a company and the necessary resources and required investments are aligned to realize the aspired goals.

Against the background of an ever increasing number of innovating technologies available and rapid pace of organisational changes, an organisation needs to have a clear vision on how best to use information technologies. A proper IT strategy is the basis to achieve this.

Defining the IT strategy from a top-down perspective is easy: the IT organisation needs to become better and cheaper. Yet, by putting this into a beautiful PowerPoint slide deck or writing it down in a nice "IT strategy" paper, the job is not done yet.

This book presents an alternative approach based on a bottom-up analysis. The required key elements for a proper IT strategy are identified and the path laid out to successfully put them into place.

In the course of taking decisions and developing activities, it is important to have the directions clear. A very wide-spread approach within the business world is the definition of a strategy. The word "strategy" comes from the Greek word *strategós* meaning *army (stratos)* and *conduct (ageîn)*. At this time, winning a battle was an issue of life and death.

© Springer Fachmedien Wiesbaden GmbH, part of Springer Nature 2018
L. Pilorget, T. Schell, *IT Management*,
https://doi.org/10.1007/978-3-658-19309-6_3

In the current economic context, the situation is less drastic. However the success of a company depends on its strategy. Thus, it is not surprising that manuscripts from famous military strategists like Sun Tzu ("The art of war" 2006) and von Clausewitz ("On War 2008") are often quoted, also in the context of IT management. Today, business intelligence, the adequacy of investments and the ability of an organisation to transform itself are key elements for "winning the battle".

The current section aims at:

- understanding the relevance of a strategy for a company
- defining the key elements of an IT strategy
- knowing how to implement an IT strategy
- understanding the complexity to put a strategy in place

3.1   Some Theories on Corporate Strategy

At this point it is interesting to reflect: "Do I know the strategy of my company?". In most cases, it is acknowledged that a company has a strategy. However, the content of the strategy is often not clear to everyone. In some organisations, the strategy may even be confidential and restricted to the top and middle management (Fig. 3.1).

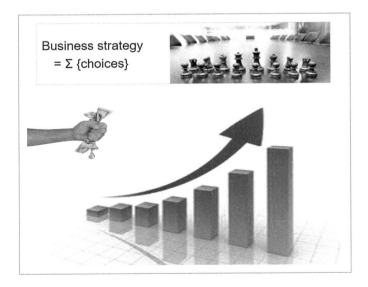

Fig. 3.1 Business Strategy = Sum of Choices

In order to have a strategy in place, it must be clear what the overall aim is. A well-spread scheme is the pyramid with the mission statement on top. At this stage, the key questions are (Fig. 3.2):

- **Vision**: why do we exist and what is important to us?
- **Mission**: what do we want to achieve and what are we willing to do?
- **Strategy**: how are we going to achieve our goals?

Knowing why you are doing what you are doing (your vision), where you intend to go and what you are willing to do for the achievement of the vision (your mission), and how you are going to do it (your strategy) is key for the development of the organisation. Therefore, dedicated activities, especially management workshops, are crucial in order to define a strategy.

Below you find an example, which illustrates the steps needed to have a strategy in place.

A company is situated at point A, and wants to reach another – more promising point, called B (see Fig. 3.3). The company may first think about the different opportunities it has. Does it choose to climb up a ladder or does it want to make a pole vault jump? It then needs to identify the resources (does the company need a trainer for the pole vault jump?). It is finally important to set up a plan and to conduct the activities planned. It is also important to check if the objective has been reached. If not, it may be useful to understand why things failed. One difficulty in "real life" is the fact that objectives may change over time. This means that point B may be removed or set at a very different place.

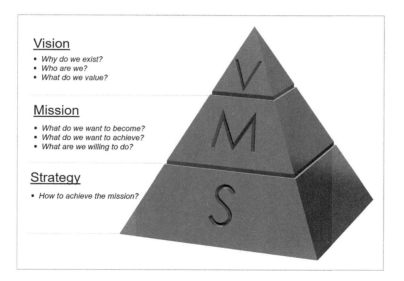

Fig. 3.2 VMS pyramid

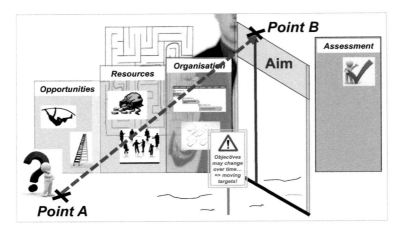

Fig. 3.3 Choosing the best strategy

It is also important to have a view on the positioning of the company. Knowing where you are and where you want to go, enables one to identify the different steps to achieve one's goal and the resources needed. A useful approach would be to conduct a SWOT analysis (strengths, weaknesses, opportunities, and threats) and to identify gaps that need to be addressed. Further strategic analyses may include a strategic segmentation including three components (Fig. 3.4):

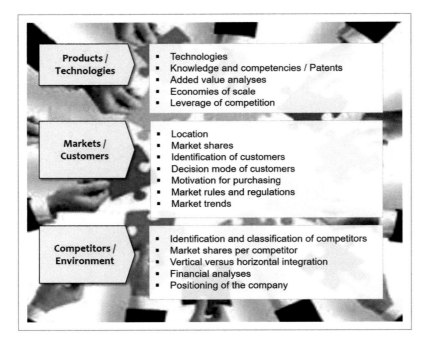

Fig. 3.4 Strategic segmentation

1. **The product and technology axis**
   This axis is about skills and competencies necessary to manufacture products and launch new ones. The question of patenting is central to protect the industrial knowledge of the company.
2. **The market and customer dimension**
   It is important to identify the target customers, in the respective countries with different channels and to find the appropriate positioning.
3. **The competitor landscape and features of the general environment**
   Being an actor of the market economy and having a good knowledge of the competitors guarantees some competitive advantages.

The literature in the field of strategy is very rich. R. Edward Freeman and M. Porter can certainly be regarded as the popes of strategic management.

Freeman has published works on the stakeholder theory, where all parties involved (including the "traditional" shareholders or stockholders but also governmental bodies, political groups, trade associations, trade unions, communities, investors, suppliers, employees, and customers) are taken into account. The idea behind his approach is to identify the principles of *who* or *what* really counts in an organisation (Fig. 3.5).

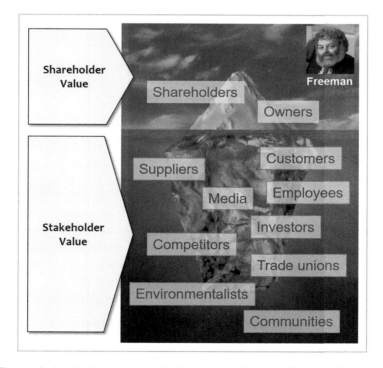

Fig. 3.5 Freeman's shareholder versus stakeholder value (see Freeman "Strategic Management 2010")

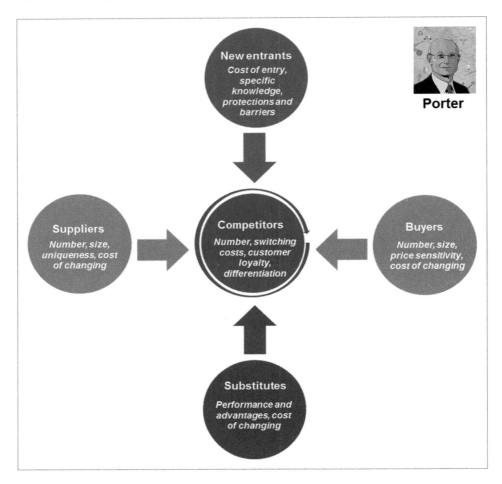

Fig. 3.6 Porter's five competitive forces (see Porter "The five competitive forces that shape strategy" 2008)

Porter defined three major strategic approaches (either cost leadership, differentiation or focus and being possibly a niche player), known as Porter's three generic strategies, which apply to any business. A company should create a competitive advantage by focusing on one of these three possible strategic behaviours. Porter takes five elements into account, which influence the development of a company (Fig. 3.6):

- **Customers (paying less to get more)**
  Buyers play an important role in defining the prices of products or services. Depending on the number of buyers, costs may change or customers switch from one provider to the other, according to their power to negotiate.

- **Suppliers (paid more to deliver less)**
  The selection of suppliers does also impact the price of products or services sold. In this context, several factors need to be taken into account, as for example the number of suppliers of each key input, the uniqueness of their components, their market strength, costs of switching from one to another etc. Again, the fewer the suppliers, the higher the dependency and the more powerful and influential the suppliers are.
- **Competitors (getting higher market shares)**
  It is important to identify competitors and to know their capability. From a market perspective, the more providers, meaning in this case the more competitors, the more difficult it will be to improve client loyalty and thus enhance profitability. In the other case, if the number of competitors is limited, the company has a good chance in garnering market shares.
- **New entrants (expanding and diversifying)**
  The ability of new companies to enter a market must also be taken into account. If the so-called barrier to entry is low (low investment, no special knowledge, no specific standards or regulation in place), the probability that new entrants appear is high. In this case, the company may have to drive prices down. If strong barriers of entry apply, the company can develop in a "secured" environment.
- **Substitutes (providing new solutions)**
  In case a product or a service may be "substituted", the company will experience difficulties to maintain market shares.

  In the event of a disruptive innovation, this situation can be very critical. The watch industry in Switzerland shows that this phenomenon is not recent (see the "quartz crisis" of the '70s, when cheap Japanese quartz watches threatened the Swiss watchmaking industry). Even although the Internet of Thing represents a new or non-predictable threat for many companies.

The world of strategic management has been largely influenced by famous consultancy companies, like the Boston Consulting Group (BCG) or Mc Kinsey. The growth–share matrix introduced by the BCG in the 1980s is a chart that helps companies to visualise their product portfolio and to determine a strategy to meet market needs (Fig. 3.7).

The matrix can be used in order to visualise the attractiveness of an area and to support analyses about the best decisions to be taken.

An increasingly important aspect in strategy deals with the factor 'innovation'. Undoubtedly Schumpeter (see Schumpeter "Essays 2004") was a pioneer when describing the process where "the opening up of new markets, foreign or domestic, and the organizational development [...] illustrate the same process of industrial

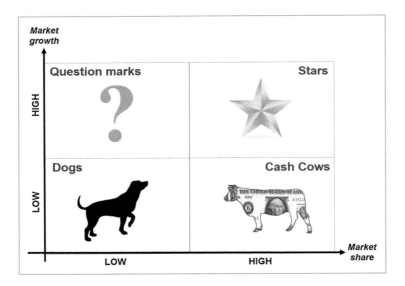

Fig. 3.7 BCG matrix

mutation, that incessantly revolutionizes the economic structure from within, incessantly destroying the old one, incessantly creating a new one". The so-called "creative destruction" process.

Even different mathematical models have been defined in order to explain and measure the diffusion of innovation or technological breakthroughs. The S-Curves emerged as a mathematical model and were afterwards applied to a variety of fields including physics, biology and economics (Fig. 3.8).

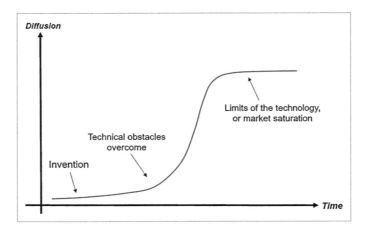

Fig. 3.8 The diffusion of innovations

3.2   IT Strategy Easily Done

It is easy to define an IT strategy from a "top-down" point of view. The aim of such an approach is to achieve one's goal in a "***better and cheaper***" way, in other words in a more efficient and effective way. One of the most memorable manners to define an IT strategy is to think of a hamburger: it is easy to eat, it looks tasty, and it is cheap and always available (Fig. 3.9).

The "hamburger" approach for defining an IT strategy might meet expectations of managers. Nevertheless, this way of proceeding may not be really sustainable for a whole company (Fig. 3.10).

With this simplistic approach, the CIO may feel like groping in the dark (Fig. 3.11). From this point of view, it would be more convenient to think about an IT strategy as a pro forma exercise, and not as a management function where conditions for providing IT services must be defined and fulfilled.

Regarding these disadvantages of the suggested approach, it becomes clear that applying a "bottom-up" view when defining an IT strategy seems more promising. The condition to be successful is to ensure the alignment between business and IT. The corresponding relevant points are going to be concisely explained in the two following chapters.

Fig. 3.9 The "hamburger" IT strategy

Fig. 3.10   The "better & cheaper" IT strategy

Fig. 3.11   The "pro forma" IT strategy exercise

3.3   Business-IT Alignment

At first glance the business-IT alignment might look like the chicken and egg problem. "IT should enable the business which should drive the IT". Or was it the other way around (Fig. 3.12)?

Many difficulties are linked to poor communication. Typically, IT would assert that business has no clue about the business needs whereas business would think that IT is not able to deliver what is needed.

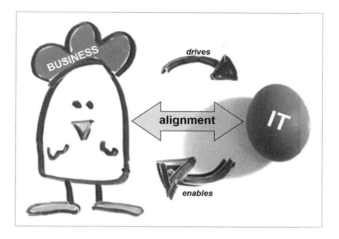

Fig. 3.12 The "chicken & egg" alignment communication between business and IT

Several behaviours can be observed on both sides which make cooperation challenging:

- business perspective on IT:
  - techno freaks
  - expensive solutions
  - self-fulfilment
  - "diva behaviour"
- IT perspective on business:
  - just do what others do
  - "golf club" relationships
  - unnecessary requirements ("green button to be implemented immediately")
  - know-it-all
  - own interests ("my son's computer does not work!")
  - no real idea and lack of vision

The IT strategy can be considered to be the wheel which ensures that a company's needs of IT deliveries are covered and properly provided by the IT organisation (Fig. 3.13).

During the development and implementation of an IT strategy, the main question remains always the same: how can IT deliver added-value to the business customer, especially if the organisation has a visible and reported strategy? The components discussed in the next section aim to answer this question.

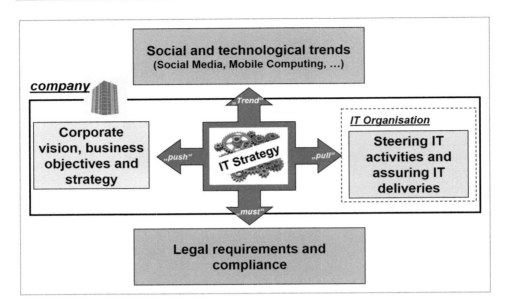

Fig. 3.13 IT strategy as a potter's wheel

3.4   The Six Key Components of an IT Strategy

One can first consider that IT strategy can be defined as a process. In order to visualise the different steps when dealing with an IT strategy, a circle can be used. The "IT Strategy Process" can thus be represented as a lifecycle (Fig. 3.14).

Four main steps are proposed:

- Identify IT needs
- Define frameworks and standards
- Communicate and implement
- Review and assess

The CIO is responsible for having the IT strategy in place, with the support of the top management and the collaboration of further IT managers, such as the IT architect, the Head of the IT Project Portfolio Management or the Head of IT Service Management.

The IT strategy should be directly related to the corporate strategy and ensure the alignment of the business needs with the delivery of IT services. Further IT processes depend on the IT strategy, especially HR management, supplier management, quality management, IT architecture & standards, the IT service management and the IT project portfolio management.

Based on the IT strategy process, it is possible to identify, in a bottom-up approach, six main components to be designed (Fig. 3.15).

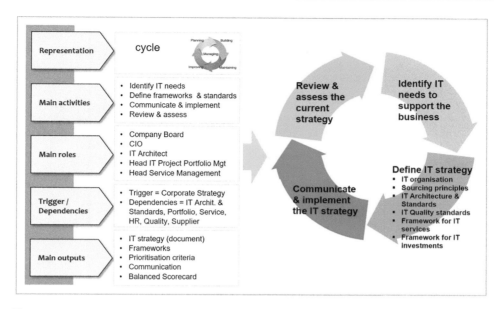

Fig. 3.14 The IT strategy lifecycle

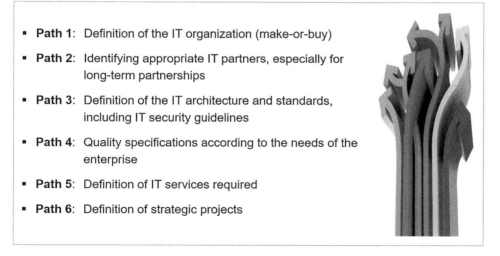

Fig. 3.15 The six major components of an IT strategy

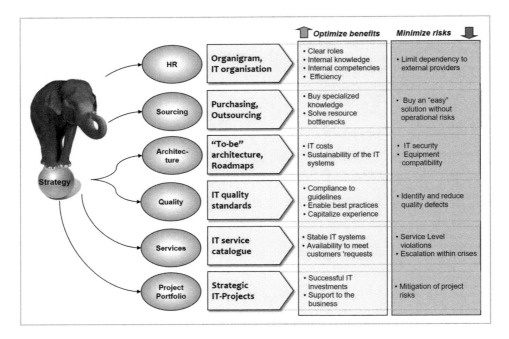

Fig. 3.16   Handling in a strategic context

These six components are essential for defining and implementing an IT strategy. They can be used as accelerator to develop the company or as a safeguard to avoid unnecessary risks (Fig. 3.16).

It is challenging to keep the balance between the above named aspects in order to take the right decisions for managing subtle situational transformations.

3.4.1   IT Personal & Organisation

Even in the case of a complete IT outsourcing, the external partner has to be managed. This means that the responsibility of managing IT remains within the organisation. In general, companies choose to set up a mix between internal and external IT resources. Having internal IT resources may enable the company to quickly set up projects with immediately available competencies and can prevent some dependencies from external providers. As a rule it might be said that an organization shall never give away the IT strategy and the governance of IT processes.

In case the internal IT has many individuals, the corresponding employees need to be managed. Depending on the approach selected by the IT management, different organigrams may apply: either a functional, a customer-orientated or a process-based one (Fig. 3.17).

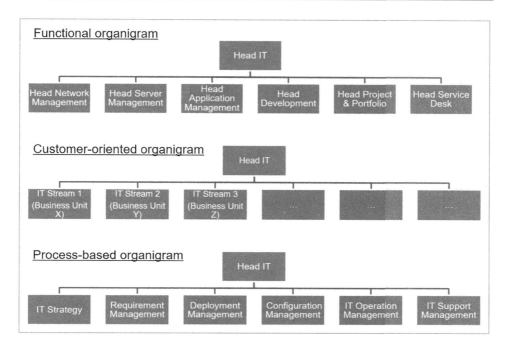

Fig. 3.17 Possible ways of defining an IT organisation

The functional approach may lead to a "silo" culture, as obviously it commonly happens in an IT organisation that the "Unix World" has nothing to do with the "Windows World" as one example. In turn, having a customer-oriented or process-based organisation would lead to a matrix organisation, where people may have difficulties to understand who is responsible for what. A mixed approach, as some kind of "hybrid solution", is often encountered.

Questions
1. Which are core IT competencies for a company?
2. Which IT competencies need to be kept and developed internally?
3. How many internal FTEs (full-time equivalent) should have the IT organisation?
4. Which organigram should be chosen?

3.4.2   Sourcing Strategy

"Make-or-Buy?": that is the question (Table 3.1).

Having internal resources in place presents many advantages. It would nevertheless be unrealistic to think that all IT services can be provided only with internal resources.

Most of the time a mix is needed, ideally 2/3 internally and 1/3 externally as a rule of thumb.

Table 3.1 Advantages and disadvantages of make or buy decisions

Option	Advantages	Disadvantages
Make	• Internal knowledge • Low priced • Highly flexible • Compliant	• Management of internal resources • Know-how increase • Coordination costs
Buy	• Focus on core competencies • "Unlimited" capacity • Highly specialised knowledge available • Somehow cheap labour • Reduced business risks • Avoidance of investments	• Price increase (especially because of contract changes) • Dependency on the external know-how • Disclosure of specific business know-how

Questions
1. Which sourcing strategy should be chosen?
2. IT Outsourcing? If yes, with whom?
3. How can risks be minimised?
4. Who are trustful external partners?
5. Who are the main providers for which business area?

3.4.3 IT Architecture & Standards

Usually, the variety of IT systems in a company is high and corresponding investments in core applications are quite subsequent. The aim of the IT architecture is to meet business requirements with IT resources, which are currently in use or need to be acquired based on technological considerations. The more specific hardware devices are, the more diversified software solutions are and the more heterogeneous IT components are in use, the more difficult and expensive it becomes to keep the "zoo" managed.

Architecture and standards can be efficient to implement cost-effective IT solutions, whereas savings on security issues should be avoided.

The IT management team should also be able to oversee the IT infrastructure and application landscape at any time. A well-developed asset and configuration management process based on a Configuration Management Database (CMDB) is key for larger organizations.

Questions
1. Which IT systems and applications are in use?
2. System map: how are the different IT systems interconnected?
3. Which IT standards are in place?
4. Which security guidelines?
5. Is a Configuration Management Database (CMDB) available?
6. Which technologies may be suitable in the future?

3.4.4   IT Quality Standards

"Quality is when the customer returns and the product doesn't", as stated by Jim Taglieber from the Miami Valley Steel Service Incorporate. Quality assurance activities focus on processes that are used to manage and deliver the IT solutions, whereas quality controls are performed continually throughout the process in order to verify that the products or the services meet the customer's expectations.

IT quality is part of the company culture, ensures compliance, and enables best practices. Maintaining high quality standards can also prevent the delivery of IT solutions with bugs which cause much trouble to the company customers, especially when time and money pressure is high (Fig. 3.18).

Managing quality is not an easy task as the customer's satisfaction depends on the perceived quality. In the software industry, this means for example to assess how easy it is to use the application. Or whether the procedure for the SW installation is convenient for the end-user.

In the car industry, the emphasis is put on the look, the touch, and the feel of a car. As the company Nissan states: "Nissan's goal is to deliver long lasting customer satisfaction through the experience of world class perceived quality of our products."

Fig. 3.18 Managing customer's expectations

Questions
1. Which quality levels must be achieved?
2. Are there industry quality standards (like Computer System Validation) that the organisation must fulfil?
3. Is an IT quality management system in place?
4. Should an ISO certification be considered?

Recommendations for Auditing Preparation
(a) Ask for a detailed list of questions well before the beginning of the audit
(b) Prepare the answers in advance and take the necessary measures in order to avoid unwanted surprises (e.g. clean up access rights)
(c) Place auditors in a quiet and separate room
(d) Manage the expectations right at the beginning of the audit in terms of goals, communication rules and the level of involvement of the employees (generate distance and respect between you and the auditors)
(e) There must only be one contact person for audit, and no direct communication between them and the rest of the company must be allowed
(f) Avoid interviews with employees who are too talkative
(g) Never provide original documents, only electronic copies
(h) Never let audit personnel work close to operations or IT, choose a segregated area with very limited access rights (e.g. client reception rooms)
(i) Limit communication with audit to an absolute minimum and by all means avoid informal discussions (lunch invitations, etc.)
(j) Answer questions as precisely and with as little information as possible
(k) Be assertive and never take risk or bluff

3.4.5   IT Service Portfolio

Internal services are needed in the process chain to manufacture products or deliver business services to the customers. Usually their range is very wide in a company: IT, HR, Facility Management, Accounting, Back Office etc.

IT services enable organisations to manage information and optimise business processes. The business needs of a company shape the definition of the required IT services. It is essential to be clear on the nature and the uniqueness of the services proposed to support the efficiency and effectiveness of the organisation.

By reason of IT services, the company can benefit from a stable and reliable environment. In case SLA violations are detected, efforts must be invested to deliver the services at a proper level.

The service portfolio includes services that are currently provided but also anticipates new services that are needed. It decommissions non-relevant services which are then phased-out and withdrawn.

Questions
1. How are IT services defined?
2. How stable do IT operations run?
3. How expensive are IT operations?
4. Is an IT service catalogue available?
5. Which new services are needed?
6. When the newest IT service was introduced in the company?

3.4.6   IT Project Portfolio

In general, many projects run in parallel in a company. The idea of the project portfolio is that projects are not managed by their own but as a bundle. Additionally, the portfolio makes sure that approved investments are in line with the strategy of the company.

The IT project portfolio guarantees that the "right" IT projects are conducted. It presents some advantages, like:

- IT investments are aligned
- risks are better managed
- resource allocation is optimised
- transparency of the anticipated investments is given
- the progress of running projects is guaranteed
- a standardised project management approach is in place
- the definition of best-practices is possible

However, this also requires a strong project management culture within the company.

Questions
1. Which projects are strategic?
2. Which criteria are used to select strategic projects?
3. Are business cases really implemented and monitored?
4. How is communication about strategic projects organised?

The aim of the project portfolio process is to choose the most valuable projects. Nevertheless, risks must be managed. Also, having too many projects with high risk profiles running in parallel may lead to a very difficult overall situation.

Literature

Freeman ER (2010) Strategic management: a stakeholder approach. Cambridge University Press, New York

Porter ME (2008) The five competitive forces that shape strategy. Harvard Business Review, Boston

Schumpeter JA (2004) Essays: on entrepreneurs, innovations, business cycles, and the evolution of capitalism. Transaction Publishers

Tzu S (2006) The art of war. Filiquarian Publishing

Von Clausewitz C (2008) On war. Wilder Publications, Radford

IT Services

4

Abstract

Employing IT service management brings many benefits, like having clear communication channels with the business or improving repeatable processes thus gaining a rewarding experience.

In addition, important psychological factors for the IT organisation are included. In general management attention tends to be concentrated on "things going wrong" and rare are the moments when "doing things right and getting the job done" are recognized or rewarded. With IT service management in place, the complexity and the interdependencies of the tasks are transparent and the perception of the services provided within the SLAs is source of pride and the basis for a trustful relationship.

This chapter presents a simple approach to have IT service management in place which enables the CSI (Continuous Service Improvement) process.

When taking a taxi to the airport, the passenger does not have to care about whether there is enough fuel in the tank or whether the cab driver has a driving licence. The person is using a service.

Services are activities where an intangible exchange of value occurs. Such as accounting, patent fees, maintenance, cleaning, consultancy, education, expertise or transports. The opposite of services are goods, which represent material properties. The boundary between goods and services is sometimes difficult to draw. By buying a bread at the bakery, the customer clearly purchases a product. Last century however, some bakers came into the neighbourhood by car and the customers rushed to the selling car to get their favourite bakery products. This example shows that many times a combination of products and services exists.

© Springer Fachmedien Wiesbaden GmbH, part of Springer Nature 2018
L. Pilorget, T. Schell, *IT Management*,
https://doi.org/10.1007/978-3-658-19309-6_4

In contrast to a product, a service cannot be stored. A service is consumed in the moment it is delivered. It does not make sense to use a taxi five times on a single Saturday in order to save time during the next business trip.

One important notion is the value of a service, which is always determined by the customer (Fig. 4.1). The recipient of a service is able to tell, whether the service delivered fulfils the needs, if the service is "good" in its perception and if it has a positive value in terms of cost/benefit perspective. One should always bear in mind that the customer always evaluates the service according to the following: individual financial benefit, perception and preferences.

Exercises

Here is a list of services. Please indicate how much you agree to pay for these services:

- Private mobile phone (costs per month)
- Hourly rate for an application expert (like in SAP field)
- Hourly rate for a strategist
- Management workshop (2 days, all-inclusive for five persons)
- Taxi ride (20 min)

An IT service can be defined as a service for the use of Information Technology in order to enable and optimise business processes for a company. The variety of IT services is quite high and having IT services in place requires a dedicated management structure (Fig. 4.2).

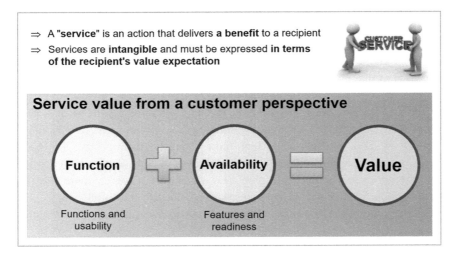

Fig. 4.1 Definition of a service and its value

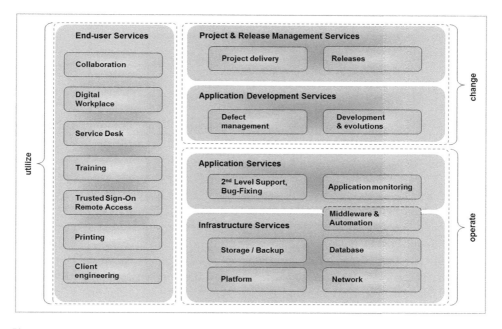

Fig. 4.2 Structure of IT services

Questions like…

• Which IT services do we need in our company?
• Which level of quality is needed?
• Who is in charge of providing the services required?
• Who is going to assess the quality and ensure the availability?
• How does the charging of the services look like?

need to find an answer. The IT Service Management (ITSM) deals with all matters concerning the needs of a company for having efficient IT services in place.

Questions
1. Which services are implemented in your company?
2. Which IT services are delivered by your IT organisation?
3. What is your perception of the IT services delivered?

The current section aims at:

• Understanding the guiding principles of service management
• Defining an IT service
• Defining and reporting a service level

- Understanding the complexity by defining IT services
- Being aware of the perceived quality
- Measuring the maturity of a service

4.1 ITSM Principles

IT Service Management (ITSM) has become a discipline in which in the meanwhile many applied theories and several tools are available. Regular battles on the question of better applicability take place between the ITIL® driven world and the DevOps advocates (DevOps is a new model for software development, where development and operations are brought together). The source of many dissensions lies in the dilemma field agility versus robustness. New agile approaches transform operations work whereas the value of collaboration between development and operations staff has become increasingly important for a service-oriented IT organisation.

Our objective is to give some simple and applicable concepts to manage IT in a company. For this reason, the ITSM presentation relates to a comprehensive framework including 4 key elements (Fig. 4.3):

- The service portfolio
- The service catalogue
- The processed services
- The Configuration Management Data Base (CMDB)

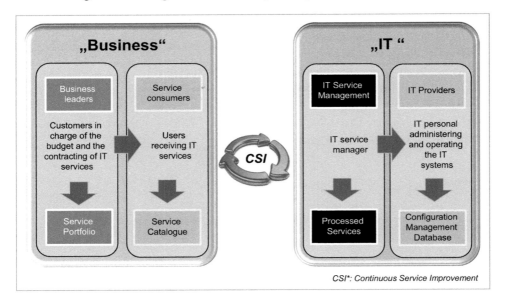

Fig. 4.3 ITSM Framework

Implementing an ITSM framework has a lot to do with the characteristics and the culture of a company. Before starting the framework definition, questions have to be answered like "Is the company organised in a strongly hierarchical way?" or "What is the highest value of the company's vision: quality, agility or innovation?".

The transformation project sponsor should know how to sell the new concept concerning service orientation and how to transform the organisation successfully. Especially the following situations or perceptions have to be considered:

- We are not defenders of a specific technology: we sell a good solution to the business
- We don't waste time: business people can save time and be more performant
- We don't want to be victims of politics: we understand the motivation of the management
- We struggle with fears and reluctance: we listen and address
- We and our customers are frustrated: we recognise and alleviate pain of our customers

It is also important to mention the ISO standard 20000, as many companies may aim at being ISO-certified.

In terms of service management and processes, the following elements, as mentioned in the ISO/IEC 20000-1:2011 service management system standard, need to be taken into account:

- **Service management system general requirements**
  - Management responsibility
  - Governance of processes operated by other parties
  - Documentation management
  - Resource management
  - Establish and improve the service management system
- **Design and transition of new or changed services**
  - Plan new or changed services
  - Design and development of new or changed services
  - Transition of new or changed services
- **Service delivery processes**
  - Service level management
  - Service reporting
  - Service continuity and availability management
  - Budgeting and accounting for services
  - Capacity management
- **Relationship processes**
  - Business relationship management
  - Supplier management

- **Resolution processes**
  - – Incident and service request management
  - – Problem management
- **Control Processes**
  - – Configuration management
  - – Change management
  - – Release and deployment management

Questions
1. Should your IT organisation have the ISO 20000 certification?
2. What would be the advantages?
3. What are the conditions that need to be met?

4.2   IT Service Portfolio

Key questions need to be answered when having services in place:

- Which (range of) services should we offer?
- How can our customers benefit from our services?
- How do we make a difference in comparison to our competitors?
- How can we create more added value for our challenging customers?
- How can we support strategic initiatives (of the customers)?
- How is it possible to make value creation visible?
- How do we define the quality of the services delivered?
- How can we take good decisions to optimise our services?
- How do we manage efficiently our limited resources?
- How can we address different needs with the same resources?

The difficulty remains the definition of an IT service itself. It should not be too specific, otherwise the list of services will be extremely long. It is important to bundle different activities, from "sub-services" to define a main service called IT service. Let's make an example: A service may be called "*workplace services*". This may include PC connectivity, remote access, outlook SW including disk space for the mailbox, disk space on file servers, printing capability and authentication.

Here are some examples of global IT services, which can be defined as standardised services:

- Directory services
- Client engineering & application service provision
- IT training services

- Customer support services
- Messaging & collaboration services
- Data centre services
- Network services
- IT architecture & infrastructure projects

Other services are more specific or may be provided locally, like:

- Application development
- Workplace support

The service portfolio aims at providing relevant services to the business (see Fig. 4.4). Therefore it includes:

- A service pipeline where new services will be proposed (for instance after the introduction of a new technology)
- Current services as described in the service catalogue
- Retired services, which are not delivered any more (old technologies, change of the needs, fusion…)

It is then important to keep the balance between supply and demand (Fig. 4.5). Therefore capacity management is key. Thanks to a price policy, it is also possible to influence the behaviour of the internal customers. In order to accelerate the decommissioning of an old technology or to promote the diffusion of a standard technology, a service may be proposed at a certain price level.

The next important element, and for the customers and users the most visible one, is the service catalogue (Fig. 4.6).

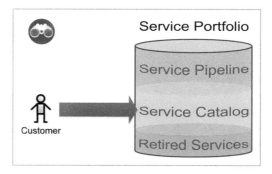

Fig. 4.4 Service portfolio lifecycle

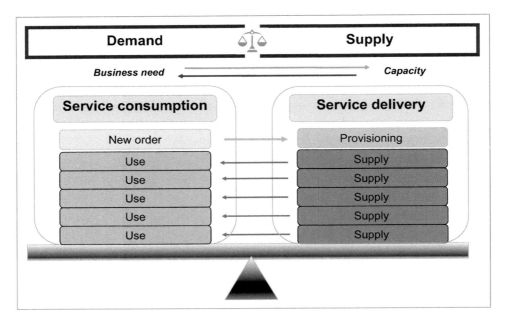

Fig. 4.5   Balancing demand and supply

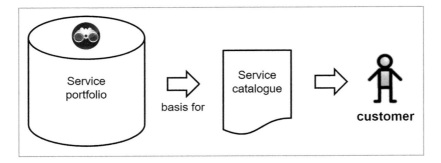

Fig. 4.6   From service portfolio to service catalogue

4.3   Service Catalogue

The service catalogue lists all IT services currently provided. It includes information like deliverables, prices, contact points and ordering processes to request the services or procedure to adjust the service reception.

In order to have services published in a service catalogue, it is important to define:

- The name of the service
- The content and the purpose
- One or more service levels (SLs), to which the service can be ordered and received, including:
  - service hours
  - support hours
  - interrupts
  - service priority
  - service quality
- Measurement metrics and KPIs

A Service Level Agreement (SLA) is an element of service management where key aspects of the service – scope, quality, responsibilities – are agreed upon between the service provider and the service recipient organisation.

An SLA Typically Includes Following Information
- Service description
- Service hours and exceptions
- Scheduled service interruptions
- Customer responsibilities
- Service provider liability and obligations
- Escalation and notification procedures
- Service targets
- Workload limits
- Details on charging
- Actions to be taken in case of incidents or disasters
- Metrics how the quality and performance can be measured
- Thresholds and criteria to check when the service is delivered as expected
- Glossary of terms

In case, the delivery of a service as defined in the SLA is not as expected, the service level is not fulfilled. This violation of the service level has to be reported. If the agreement is made as an underpinning contract, penalties will have to be payed as damage compensations.

Most service providers offer different service levels, which differ in performance or support, and perhaps also in quality. An agreement may state that the service level has to be higher during office hours, lower during the rest of the time. The working week is normally divided into three categories of service time (Fig. 4.7).

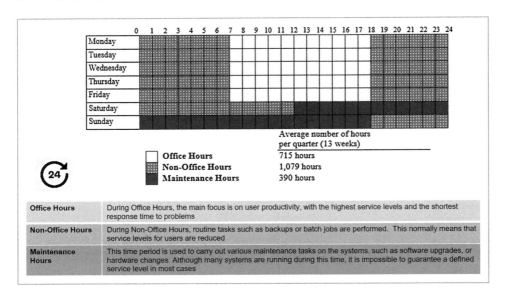

Fig. 4.7 Definition of service hours

A service level is specified for a time period. "Planned interrupts" are long term changes. All other interrupts are known as "unplanned interrupts".

The **availability** of a service can be defined as followed:

$$Availability = 1 - \frac{planned + unplanned\ interrupts\ per\ period}{Number\ of\ service\ hours\ per\ period}$$

Here is an example for a service where two planned interrupts of 1 h are agreed and maximum two unplanned interrupts of 1 h are tolerated.

The minimum availability to be guaranteed is:

$$Availability\ (during\ office\ hours) = 1 - \frac{2*1 + 1*2}{1079} = 99.6\%$$

The **Business Importance Level** (BIL) indicates the importance of a service to the customer's business. Thanks to this definition, the customer expresses in which way the service will influence the business processes, and especially in case of a service interruption. Hence the BIL is specified in every item of the service catalogue. The BIL is used to determine the priority of a call ticket after its impact level has been selected.

The following four business importance levels will be presented to differentiate between the business meaning of services for customers:

- **Core**
- **Critical**
- **Important**
- **Useful**

The impact defines the extent to which the functionality or the performance of a service is classified. The impact becomes greater as the functionality of the service is operated in a degraded mode and/or more users are affected.

The following impact levels are referred to:

- **High**: Service down for several users
- **Medium**: Service down for one user or service degradation for several users
- **Low**: Service degradation for one user
- **None**: No degradation of service

The impact, in combination with the BIL, is used to determine the priority of call tickets.

Table 4.1 shows the priority levels that correspond to the different impact/BIL combinations.

Table 4.1 *Definition of the service* business importance level (BIL)

		Business importance level			
		Core	Critical	Important	Useful
Impact	**High**	catastrophic	very high	medium	low
	Medium	very high	high	medium	low
	Low	medium	medium	very low	very low
	None	low	low	very low	marginal

  1. Do you have an IT service catalogue in place?
  2. How many pages?
  3. Is each service description clear and understandable?

4.4   Process-to-Service

Once services are identified and defined within the service catalogue, the delivery of the contracted services takes place (Table 4.2). It follows a circle with four different steps (Fig. 4.8):

• Service definition in the service catalogue
• Contracting
• Delivery and monitoring
• Charging and reporting

Within the service-providing organisation, the correct delivery of services requires (Fig. 4.9):

(a) The identification of processes needed
(b) The identification and provisioning of adequate skills
(c) The integration of the delivered service into existing tools and process management systems
(d) The management of supplier relations

Depending on the specificity of the environment and the exclusivity of the services, it may be quite challenging to have all services provided (Fig. 4.10). Especially if the business needs are very heterogeneous.

In order to manage the complexity of providing IT services or in order to avoid contracts where service levels cannot be fulfilled, it may be useful to add an intermediate level and defined so-called **operational-level agreements (OLA)**, which govern the interdependent relationships between the different internal actors needed to have fully operated services in place (Fig. 4.11).

  1. How many services does your IT deliver?
  2. How many employees belong to the IT organisation?
  3. How many external suppliers are needed?
  4. How many different customers are receiving IT services?

Table 4.2 Service management steps

A) Service catalogue	Different types of services are proposed, especially: • Standard services/operations which are services provided to all business functions, e.g. workplace support or collaboration services • Dedicated services, which are contracted with the respective business functions, for example a business application with particular functionality for a business unit Each year, the service portfolio is adjusted in response to changing business requirements and technical innovations. Detailed descriptions of services, service groups or bundles, service levels, and prices or charging schemes are provided
B) Service contracting	Contracting may take place once per year as part of the annual budgeting process Service contracting for standard services should be completed on the basis of the regular usage of services. Rules for charging within a corporate organisation need to be defined (what is charged locally and what is relevant at corporate level). It is recommended to do a quarterly review of the IT services that are consumed by each business unit compared to the contracted volume. Extra charges for services that are consumed and which have not been contracted will be applied and if necessary this will lead to a re-negotiation of contracts The contracts specify the expected requirements for IT services, in terms of quantities and values. They are based on volumes that the customer realistically expects. Both parties must sign the contracts. IT uses this data as the basis for resource planning. As a basic principle, contracted services take precedence over non-contracted requirements. During the contracting phase, business functions should specify their particular requirements for IT manpower. Long-term manpower requirements should be communicated. IT carries out manpower planning on the basis of these requests. If investments are made in new infrastructure, which will be provided in response to a customer's request, then the customer will be charged for instance over a 3-year period, as long as the infrastructure is not used for any other purpose
C) Delivery and monitoring	IT provides the contracted volumes of services required in conformity with the price and quality conditions as described in the service catalogues (or in special contracts). If the actual demand exceeds the contracted volume during the contract period, IT will make every effort to cover the additional requirements (but without guarantee) IT has to give the guarantee that all processes developed to deliver the best services are documented, implemented, reviewed, and improved. It is also important to make sure that the quality management system ensures compliancy with the corporate rules (for instance regarding Computer System Validation for the pharma industry)
D) Charging and reporting	In order to allow an optimal allocation of resources, the consumption of IT services needs to be mapped in the financial controlling systems. There, service costs as standard unit prices multiplied with consumed quantities per period are invoiced by the service provider. The fixed IT service contract debits the business areas with the contract being periodically reviewed against service consumption (best: quarterly) The objective of IT is also to inform the customers about the actual quality and usage of the services provided. Two kinds of reports are useful (on a quarterly basis): • **Service reports**, detailing information about the actual quality of the provided services, for allowing a comparison with the contracted quality (standard service levels) as described in the service catalogue • **Usage/volume reports**, detailing information on the actual volumes/usage, for enabling comparison with the contracted volumes and costs

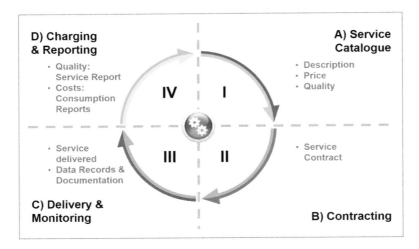

Fig. 4.8 Service management wheel

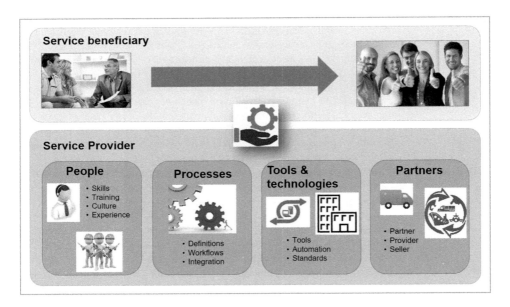

Fig. 4.9 Providing services (people, processes, tool & technologies and partners)

Keeping the balance between needs and delivery remains a major accomplishment, which requires commitment, mutual understanding and performance eagerness (Fig. 4.12).

Before closing this section, some examples about ITSM reporting are included.

The diagram (Chart 4.1) shows the response rate of the end-user support on quarterly basis over a period of 2 years.

The service level stipulates that at least 75% of all calls should be directly solved by the service desk.

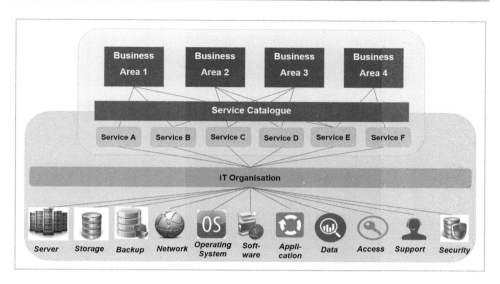

Fig. 4.10 Service catalogue as an interface between business and IT

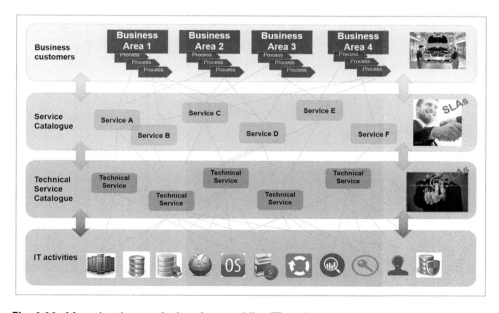

Fig. 4.11 Managing the complexity when providing IT services

The fact that the service level was not reached over a period of nearly 6 months should require an analysis. It may have been that this insufficient performance was caused by the introduction of a new operating system for workplaces. However, it is important to send a report to the decision makers only with an interpretation of the reporting results explaining why service level violations took place.

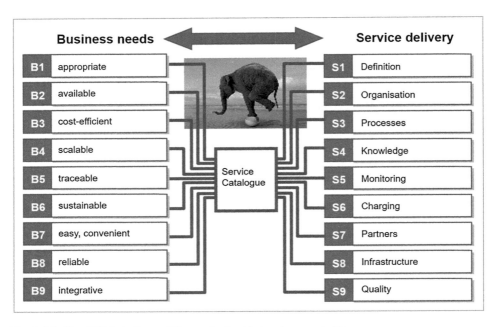

Fig. 4.12 The ITSM challenge (like an elephant balancing on a ball)

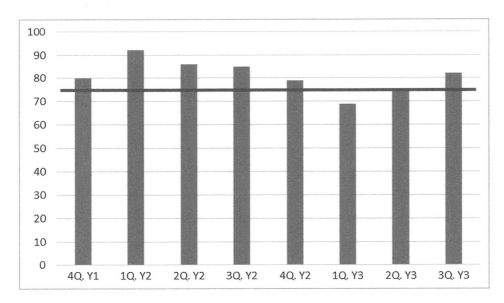

Chart 4.1 Response rate of the end-user support

The following chart (Chart 4.2) shows the feedbacks collected via questionnaire once a training session has been delivered. The aim is to have a satisfaction level of challenging 95%.

The following graph (Chart 4.3) shows the system availability overall and during office hours on a quarterly basis.

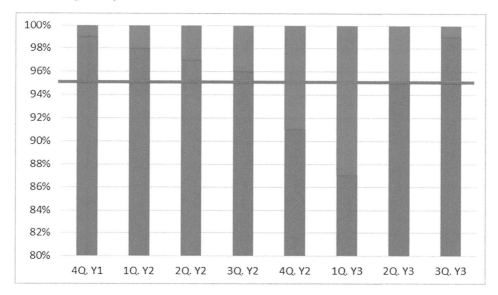

Chart 4.2   Feedback collection via questionnaire

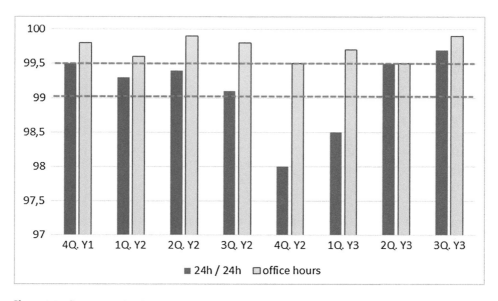

Chart 4.3   System availability

An availability of at least 99.50% is required during office hours. Overall an availability of 99% is expected. This example shows that the SLA during office hours has been fulfilled whereas service violations were noticed on an overall basis.

4.5   Configuration Management Data Base (CMDB)

IT provides information technology for provisioning or processing services to customers. In many situations, IT does not have the information at hand that is urgently needed for own purposes. For instance questions like *"how many servers are operated?"* or *"do we need more licenses?"* cannot be answered immediately.

According to Wikipedia, *"a **Configuration Management Database (CMDB)** is a repository that acts as a data warehouse for information technology (IT) organizations. Its contents are intended to hold a collection of IT assets that are commonly referred to as configuration items (CI), as well as descriptive relationships between such assets"*.

As mentioned by Gartner, *"the **CMDB** focuses on the physical rather than intangible fulfilment elements of a service and is more aligned to service change and execution, rather than service prioritization and planning"*.

The CMDB can be first defined as a collection of information data, so-called configuration items, like the following ones:

*   Name
*   Description
*   Person in charge
*   Category (e.g. hardware, software, account …)
*   Type (e.g. server, printer …)
*   Manufacturer information
*   Version
*   Modification history
*   Status history
*   Relationships to IT services
*   Relationships to other CIs
*   Relationships to documents
*   Relationships to users

The information tags of a configuration item can be summarised as "CARS": Category, Attributes, Relations, and Status.

Having a CMDB in place requires different steps as illustrated in Table 4.3.

The CMDB is an important source of information and is used as a repository to centralise and permanently collect valuable data for many IT processes as illustrated in the Fig. 4.13.

Table 4.3 Having a CMDB in place

Planning	**Planning** Define the data within a CMDB. Which categories and CI types shall be available for the grouping and categorisation of the configuration items? Which attributes per CI category, which relations, and status values in general will be used? Define roles and responsibilities for the management of the CMDB and its relations and interfaces. How will the timeliness and correctness of data be guaranteed and measured? Which reports out of the CMDB will be needed within the next 3–6 months and which will be established later? How will the CMDB contribute to a general IT management dashboard?
Identifi-cation	**Identification** At this stage, the CMDB will be initially populated with the elements in the IT infrastructure. For each CI category, items will be identified by stock-taking and will be labelled with a single CI name, which acts as unique identifier Software licenses are summarised from given contracts, and installed software scanned on all workstations of IT users. Business applications are listed. Databases, servers and network elements are indexed by means of electronic measures or manually For all CI categories and types the defined attributes are filled with real values found. CI documentation, ownership, and responsible persons will be identified CIs should be recorded at a level of detail justified by the business need, typically to the level of "independent change". This includes defining the relationships of the CIs in the system
Control	**Control** This step will assure that only authorised and identifiable CIs are accepted and recorded from receipt to disposal. It ensures that no CI is added, modified, replaced or removed without the appropriate controlling documentation e.g. approved requests for change of a CI or an updated specification
Monitoring	**Monitoring** The correctness and the timeliness of the CMDB content will be controlled permanently or regularly with appropriate metrics and measurement methods Technical measures will be used, e.g. a server in status "live" shall answer a network ping. An IT user who has left the company should not have any IT equipment related, etc Monitoring results are used for the provisioning of statistical records and contribute to IT management dashboards, which can also be used for the service charging to customers
Verifi-cation	**Verification** Even with a "perfect" controlling, it will become necessary to verify the physical existence of CIs, and to check that they are correctly recorded in the CMDB and parts list This is done by reviews, audits, samples and regular stock-takings in offices, stock rooms, and data centres

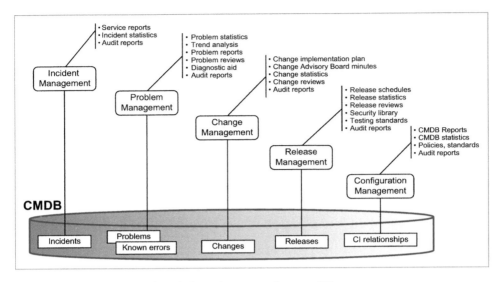

Fig. 4.13 CMDB as a repository information source for many IT processes

Questions
- Is a CMDB in use in your organisation? For which purposes?
- CMDB in the clouds: What is your opinion? Why?

4.6   Continuous Service Improvement (CSI) & Service Maturity

Based on a regular review of IT services, service quality can be improved where necessary. In addition more efficient ways of providing a service can be identified. Many methods and metrics (like regular benchmarks, audits and maturity assessments) can be used to identify improvement areas.

Specific initiatives to improve IT services and processes can be launched. It is important to:

- track the activities in order to check if the improvement initiatives are conducted according to plan
- to identify additional measures if needed
- to make continuous improvement in all areas of service operation and delivery as a proactive part of the culture in the service provider organisation

A simple method to illustrate this approach is the Deming- or PDCA-cycle that is shown in Fig. 4.14 (see Deming "Out of the crisis" 1982):

- **Plan**: Define the objectives to be achieved and specify the targeted improvements
- **Do**: Execute the plan and implement

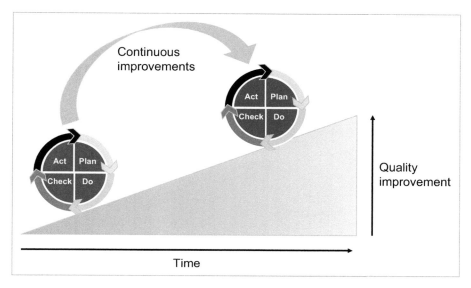

Continuous
improvements

Quality
improvement

Time

Fig. 4.14   The P-D-C-A cycle (Plan - Do - Check - Act)

- **Check**: Collect data to measure the actual results and compare against the expected ones
- **Act**: a new standard baseline has to be defined if the quality improvement measures have been successfully conducted and a new cycle can start. In case objectives are not reached, the situation needs to be analysed and learnings should be done.

The Deming cycle is a well-established method in various industries.

Another interesting model is the maturity model, which allows best management practice.

The **Capability Maturity Model Integration** (**CMMI**) is a programme administered and marketed by the Carnegie Mellon University. When defining the level to be reached for a service and the current situation, gaps can be precisely identified and measures needed can be suggested to the management (Fig. 4.15).

An important aspect in the service area deals with the perception of quality. As stated by Shiro Nakamura, Nissan Chief Creative Officer, in the field of car manufacturing.

Nissan defines perceived quality as such:

The term "Perceived Quality" refers to the quality that customers acknowledge via the look, the touch, and the feel of a car. For example, in a showroom, the customer would first take a glance around the car, then open the door, sit on the seat, and check the quality of the details. At Nissan, we are systematically working on techniques to enhance both the quality feel and the craftsmanship perceivable through the five senses.

When some easy ideas are implemented, this can immediately change the perception of the IT organisation in a positive manner:

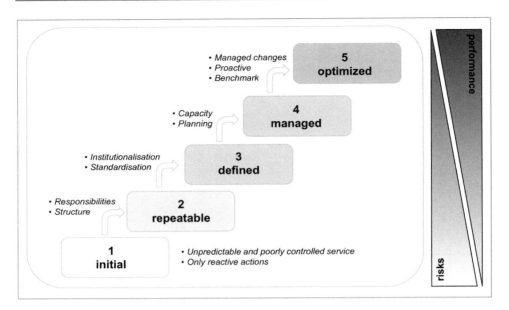

Fig. 4.15 The maturity model applied to IT services

- Let customers get to know you
- Be available and present
- Provide excellent support
- Inform proactively during interruptions
- Provide special/VIP services
- Provide knowledge to user support and customers
- Enable community platforms

Successful ITSM
- Understand your requirements
- Separate the "wants from the needs." Define what will truly generate value for your company
- Think of tools as strategic partners
- Think of tools within the context of "applications that execute functionality" is a mistake
- View ITSM as a relationship not a line item
- Most ITSM tool acquisitions are one of the higher IT-related expenditures for an organisation. The tool, however, is only the beginning. Enterprises are also entering into a long-term relationship with the vendor. Be certain the vendor is a good fit for the organisation

- Evaluate ease of migration and integration
- Organisations that have locked themselves into customised solutions often under-estimate what it will take to migrate information and integrate tools
- Validate through certification
- Review ITSM certifications and ratings to determine if a product is meeting compliance standards or adhering to ITSM best practices
- Ensure workflow integration
- The synergy of integrated process automation within ITSM tools should be a strong criteria for the final tool selection
- Adhere to legislation requirements
- Legislative mandates on information and the tools that manage such data need to be considered when evaluating an ITSM solution
- Assess delivery models
- Companies are able to choose from a SaaS-based (Software as a Service) or on premise ITSM deployment. Each has special considerations for your business. Take the time to determine what makes the most sense
- Beware of common traps
- Do not fall victim to false statements such as: "Greater product sophistication means a better ROI" or "There is no such thing as out-of-the box"
- Find the right solution – generate a strong ROI
- ITSM tools can provide an increase in ROI and positively affect cost of ownership. Not only can the right ITSM tool pay for itself in less than a year or two, it can drive down costs in other areas of your organisation through cost and risk avoidance in administration, operational overhead, training and just about every other cost centre of the IT budget

Source: www.zdnet.com

Literature

Deming EW (1982) Out of the crisis. Massachusetts Institute of Technology, Cambridge
Pilorget L (2015) Implementing IT processes. Springer, Wiesbaden

IT Portfolio and Project Management

5

Abstract

It is easy to reduce IT expenditures, just by decreasing IT investments. On the long term, this is not a viable approach as a firm has to continuously invest in IT, firstly to maintain the IT assets in terms of life cycle and secondly to introduce new technologies to keep pace with complex and moving markets.

So the two questions to be answered are: in which IT areas should a company invest and how should the corresponding investments be managed?

The IT project portfolio management process and the IT project management guidelines give an answer to these two questions and are presented in the following chapter.

Especially a project methodology is introduced based on a phased model. This approach is compatible with different project delivery strategies like waterfall, scrump or iterative development processes. The proposed structure allows a robust and down-to-earth practice to conduct projects in a safe way, including all aspects of project management like risk management, planning or communication.

5.1   Introduction

As a matter of fact, projects are part of companies' everyday life. However, projects are different in nature, objectives and context. Project activities can vary from launching a new product, conducting due diligence activities or implementing a new IT solution.

The way of managing projects depends on the culture of the company. Usually, many projects are running in parallel. To keep overview on resources, time and plans, organisations run projects with a multi-project management which allows to consider even the interdependencies between projects. In some cases, portfolio management may be used, especially if several strategic initiatives run in parallel and therefore prioritisation, resource allocation, deadlines, risks and opportunities need to be streamlined and managed (Fig. 5.1).

© Springer Fachmedien Wiesbaden GmbH, part of Springer Nature 2018
L. Pilorget, T. Schell, *IT Management*,
https://doi.org/10.1007/978-3-658-19309-6_5

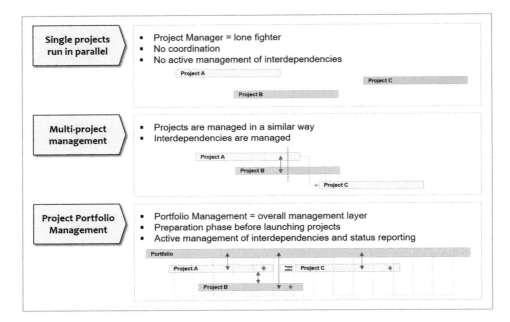

Fig. 5.1 Company governance to manage projects

Example: The IT organisation of a medium-size company has to upgrade the operating system on all PCs, introduce a new CRM (Customer Relationship Management) solution for the sales department and is still implementing ITSM processes with a new ticketing system for incident and change management. There are only limited resources concurrently occupied by operational tasks.

Multi-project management would provide a clear resource allocation and would shift project timelines according to the resource availabilities. Portfolio management would – probably – start with the introduction of a small function for the operation of daily tasks like monitoring, back-up, job-control, etc. With this new function the IT-resources needed for the major projects would be released.

Two key questions have to be answered in the context of IT investments:

1. What are the "right" projects for the company, in the sense of being valuable for the company? (Portfolio)
2. How projects are implemented and executed the "right" way? (Project management method)

The first question refers to a typical portfolio-oriented topic and will be answered in the following section. To answer the second one, an "home-made" IT project management methodology will be proposed.

This chapter aims at:

• Being able to identify strategic projects
• Being able to define criteria in order to prioritise requirements
• Defining a business case for IT projects

- Applying a project management method
- Understanding the different roles in a project
- Understanding the importance of the human dimension in a change process

5.2   IT Project Portfolio Management

The following section will answer the following question: What are the most valuable IT projects for a company (Fig. 5.2)?

An IT project portfolio management is usually set up in order to perform optimal use of deployment activities in a company's IT area. Based on a global recurring procedure, the project portfolio process will enable a company to make the right selection of IT projects. The project portfolio also constitutes a management tool to plan and coordinate projects on a global level. This includes the choice and introduction of software solutions, the use of synergies and benchmark studies and the optimal management of internal and external resources.

The following preconditions need to apply when an IT project portfolio shall run optimally:

1. Processes or functions are in place understanding the business needs and are able to identify the functionalities that add most value to the customer
2. IT investment for projects is done yearly according to the budget targets
3. Critical Success Factors (CSFs) are defined in accordance to the business strategy to guarantee strategic alignment
4. The management approval process is done at a centralised global level and not for each project separately
5. Projects are run company-wide according to an approved project management methodology and reporting activities will be organised according to the governance structure
6. Benefit tracking is seen as an important evaluation activity and is run by the business in co-operation with IT responsible authorities

Fig. 5.2 The most valuable IT projects for the company

5.2.1   IT Project Portfolio Recurring Process

The project portfolio can be defined as a process. Many representations can be used. Below a representation in form of a cycle is depicted in Fig. 5.3.

Sometimes the portfolio process is represented as a double helix, where the duality of the portfolio activities can be represented. In the following picture a Mobius strip is used to visualise this duality (Fig. 5.4).

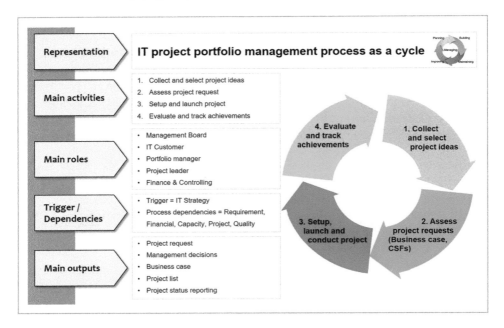

Fig. 5.3   IT project portfolio process as a cycle

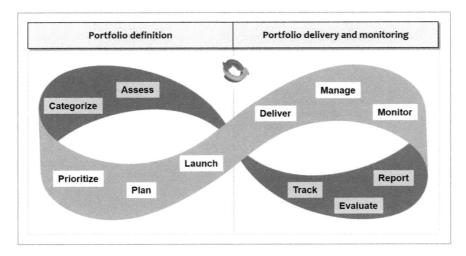

Fig. 5.4   The duality of project portfolio

In order to represent the project portfolio process, the following model based on four major steps may be used as described in the Fig. 5.5.

The four steps are:

- Step 1: Collect and select project ideas
- Step 2: Assess project requests
- Step 3: Setup, launch and monitor projects
- Step 4: Evaluate achievements

5.2.2   Step 1: Collect and Select Project Ideas

The first step deals with collecting and selecting project ideas and needs of future IT deployments. This is either initiated by the business or the IT community. It has to be consolidated **by both** in order to get jointly scoped IT solutions.

Often, IT is called by business customers to provide a "solution" in order to "fulfil" the needs of an already designed and planned business process. Sometimes even, business has purchased already some external software asking IT afterwards to integrate it into the given service or application portfolio.

Ideally, IT has a place on the round-table, where a new business process is designed and can offer services already in the very beginning of the process design.

Example: the customer asks for two servers and a database. A "small" software application for "competition management" has been purchased and the business wants to have this new application integrated with the company's CRM-solution. The IT account manager needs to know that the company's ERP (Enterprise Resource Planning) system includes already a competition management module in the existing license fees.

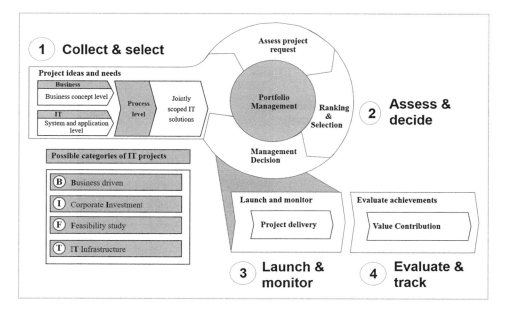

Fig. 5.5 Four major steps in IT project portfolio

The role or function of a business relation management on strategic and tactical levels helps a company to use existing resource in a higher integrated and therefore more effective way. It avoids duplication of effort and supports a long-term planning of resources and IT demands.

Beside the business demand, many sources can be relevant in order to generate ideas for IT improvements. For instance:

- Corporate strategic initiatives
- Wishes from board members
- Market needs to develop new business areas
- Offering from external suppliers
- Compliance requirements
- Long-term investment policies
- Customer complaints
- Technological evolution
- Equipment lifecycle
- Merges & acquisitions
- Process improvements to reduce manufacturing costs

Exercises

List the main sources of idea generation for business and/or IT investments in your company:

- ...
- ...
- ...

At this stage it is helpful to define project categories. For instance:

- **Business driven projects**
  Business units initiate IT projects in order to improve their performance. This means for instance to automate business processes or to increase quality for customers. The business case is not IT specific and is part of the overall business strategy.
- **Corporate investment projects**
  IT projects that are linked to business investments. A classic example is the implementation of a new SAP solution when a new factory is built. Here again, the business case for the IT part is included in the overall business strategy.
- **Feasibility study projects**
  Feasibility studies are conducted to evaluate business opportunities of strategic importance. The result is to decide on the usefulness of further investments.
- **IT Infrastructure projects**
  These projects deal with the IT infrastructure, either to implement new infrastructure elements or to upgrade existing ones in terms of system lifecycle.

Below, different information needs that have to be collected in order to properly understand the business intent are listed in Fig. 5.6.

Project request

Business Problem or Opportunity
- Description of current situation
- Description of the current problem and the potential impact on customers
- Indication about the quantitative magnitude of the improvement idea

Improvement Objectives
- Status to be achieved once the project is done
- Description of the new situation to be reached
- Impact on customers

Strategic relevance and potential benefits
- Link to the corporate strategy
- Benefits for the company and the strategic contribution

Project delivery and deliverables • Design of the way to achieve the objectives • Definition of the deliverables	**Financial analysis** • Rough estimation of costs • Possible estimation of savings or increase of revenues
Project boundaries • Definition of the scope of the potential project • Precise activities out-of-scope	**Stakeholders, Sponsor and competencies needed** • Persons or entities with a real interest for the improvement • List of persons or entities to be involved
Frame conditions • Definition of the critical success factors	**Expected Timeline** • Precise deadlines to be met
Category and dependencies • Project category • Main dependencies	**Risks** • Main risks identified until now • Risk mitigation measures to be taken

Fig. 5.6 Drafting a project request

It is important to gather information concerning the following topics and to develop a good understanding of the intention of the planned project:

- **Business Problem/Opportunity**
  - Description of the current situation
  - Description of the current issues and risks and the potential impact on customers (if the current situation does not have any disadvantages, no improvement is needed)
  - Indication about the quantitative magnitude of the improvement idea
- **Improvement Objectives**
  - Status to be achieved once the project is finalised
  - Description of the new situation, which can be reached with the project
  - Impact on customers
- **Strategic relevance and potential benefits**
  - Link to the corporate strategy. In which way the improvement is linked to the overall vision?
  - Benefits for the company and the strategic contribution
- **Project delivery and deliverables**
  - The way to achieve the objectives
  - Definition of the deliverables
- **Project boundaries**
  - Definition of the scope of the potential project
  - Precise activities out-of-scope

- **Frame conditions**
  - Definition of the critical success factors
- **Category and dependencies**
  - Project category
  - Main dependencies
- **Financial analysis**
  - Rough estimation of costs
  - If possible, an estimation of savings or increase of revenues
- **Stakeholders, sponsor and competencies needed**
  - Persons or entities with a real interest for the improvement
  - List of persons or entities to be involved
- **Expected timeline**
  - Precise deadlines to be met
- **Risks**
  - Main risks identified so far
  - Risk mitigation measures to be taken

A risk profile may be defined in order to assess the chance of success, especially concerning:

- Skills & resources
- Time & planning
- Budget & costs
- Business impact, especially on customers

Each area can be assessed (1 point for low risk, 2 points for medium risk and 3 points for high risk). The following table shows in an exemplary way the rules for the assessment of the different risk areas (Table 5.1):

Table 5.1 Assessment of risk profile

	Low	Medium	High
	1 point	*2 points*	*3 points*
Skills resources	Know-how and resources available	Know-how and resources not completely available	Important know-how and resources missing
Time planning	< 6 Months, or low time pressure	> 6 Months, time pressure	> 6 Months High time pressure
Budget costs	< 0.5 Mio USD	> 0.5 Mio USD	> 2.0 Mio USD
Business impact	Low business risks	Middle business risk or medium strategic importance	High business risk or high strategic importance
Total	Sum of points given		

Based on the risk assessment, three types of risk profiles can be defined:

- **high** : total = 10–12 points
- **medium** : total = 6–9 points
- **low** : total = 4–5 points

Requests have to be sent to an overall corporate unit where proposals are registered and checked. This is necessary to avoid redundancies and to make sure that the requests are clear and understandable.

Below an example of a check list is depicted, which helps to make sure that all relevant information is available before the start of the project.

Check List

Value benefit analysis

- Is the request mandatory? Why?   ☐
- Estimate of potential benefits? Under which conditions ?   ☐
- Are the costs for the planned investment "affordable" ?   ☐
- Is an estimate of internal efforts available ?   ☐

Solution proposal

- Does a solution exist in another entity?   ☐
- Is a solution provided by corporate core IT systems?   ☐
- Do other companies have the same problem? How is it solved?   ☐
- Who are the external providers to be contacted?   ☐
- Is outsourcing a possible answer?   ☐

Impact onproducts and channels

- Which products are impacted ?   ☐
- Which customers are impacted?   ☐
- Are there impacts on customer channels?   ☐

Impact on organisation and processes

- Which processes are impacted?   ☐
- Which process descriptions need to be actualised?   ☐
- Which organisational units need to be involved ?   ☐
- Which guidelines and policies need to be actualised?   ☐
- Which impact on cross-divisional departments, like accounting, could arise?   ☐
- Is there an impact on compliance rules? How?   ☐
- Is there any impact on the company's governance?   ☐

Impact on Security and IT systems

- Do security aspects need to be taken into account?   ☐
- Do security standards need to be amended?   ☐
- Which IT systems need to be taken into account ?   ☐
- What are the side-effects on existing services or systems?   ☐

5.2.3   Step 2: Assess Project Requests

This step constitutes the entry into the project portfolio and the beginning of the decision process. Two major analysis methods can be used in order to rank and select IT projects:

- Cost/Benefit information, or so-called Business Cases
- Strategic alignment based on Critical Success Factors (CSFs) assessment

5.2.3.1 Business Case for IT Investments
The business case is a management instrument to take decisions.

Given several assumptions, different information pieces are collected and quantified to weigh the benefits and risks for an IT investment. It is recommended to have alternative scenarios (a "plan B") and the commitment of the management at all levels.

Most business cases are based on an estimate of the costs and the expected revenues. Different accounting methods may be used, like the Net Present Value (NPV). This helps to evaluate the profitability of a projected investment by calculating the difference between net cash inflows during a certain period taking a discount rate into account and the total initial investment costs.

Project costs should be calculated according to the corporate financial guidelines.

Project costs comprise:

- Internal IT staff (local or headquarters)
- External IT staff
- External back-filling staff for business
- Hardware expenses (calculation based on depreciation)
- Software costs (licenses)
- Others (travel expenses, project rooms etc.)

The cash-out part includes the project costs minus the costs for internal IT staff and is known most of the time as the project budget.

Based on a Total Costs of Ownership (TCO) approach, **operational costs** for the operation of the project deliverables should also be taken into account. This applies to the incremental costs only and includes:

- Internal IT staff (local or headquarters)
- External IT staff
- Business staff
- Hardware depreciation
- Hardware and Software maintenance
- Others (travel expenses, facilities, etc.)

Tangible benefits for the business and the IT area should also be calculated:

Business
- Headcount reduction
- Operating cost reduction
- Additional profit generation
- Others

IT
- Headcount reduction
- Operating cost reduction
- System replacement
- Others

Cost avoidance may also be taken into account in order to assess investments. This is the case when some extra-activities to be done in the future will be avoided once the project is closed. One example is when merging different IT systems, the maintenance and support activities needed for the multiple systems can be avoided which means that the corresponding costs per system can be saved.

Intangible benefits are benefits, which cannot be easily assessed monetarily. A typical example would be the claim to aim for a better decision-making process (Fig. 5.7).

The return on investment, called ROI, is calculated most of the time based on:

ROI = [Tangible Benefits / TCO]*100
TCO = Project costs (excluding internal IT staff) + incremental operational costs

An extended return on investment can calculated based on:

ROI extended = [Benefits / TCO]*100
Benefits extended = Tangible and intangible Benefits
TCO extended = Project costs (including internal IT staff) + incremental operational costs

Costs	Y	Y+1	Y+2	Y+2	Y+3	Total
Internal Manpower						
External consultancy						
HW						
SW						
Others (Travel,…)						
Incremental Costs						
Benefits	**Y**	**Y+1**	**Y+2**	**Y+2**	**Y+3**	**Total**
Headcount reduction						
Operating cost reduction						
Additional profit generation						
Others						
System replacement						
Cost avoidance						

Fig. 5.7   Calculating a business case for an IT investment

The payback calculation provides the time needed, calculated in years, to reach the break-even point. It gives an idea on the point in time when the investment pays off, providing the benefits increase with time. As the IT technologies develop quite quickly, it is certainly recommended to consider less than a 2-year payback for an IT project.

Depending on the size and the category of the project proposed, it may not be needed to calculate a business case. For instance a lifecycle-based IT investment required for a critical application does not need a business case as risks are too high if the application is not available anymore. In the case of a mandatory project for compliance reasons, the question of the business case is also not relevant.

5.2.3.2 Strategic Value of IT Investments Based on CSFs

The Critical Success Factors (CSFs) assessment is conducted in order to guarantee that the IT projects proposed are in line with the corporate business strategy and support the strategic direction in an optimal way.

Exercises

Please define the CSFs, according to the strategy of your company, to select appropriate IT investments?

- …
- …
- …

The assessment can be based on two basic questions, leading to 10 critical success factors Fig. 5.8):

Does the project support growth?	High (4 points)	Medium (2 points)	Low (1 point)	zero
1. Add new business (new products or new customers)?				
2. Increase customer value (more sales or value for customers)?				
3. Increase existing customer binding?				
4. Increase production flexibility?				
5. Create an unique sustainable competitive advantage?				
Does the project enable cost effectiveness?	High (4 points)	Medium (2 points)	Low (1 point)	zero
6. Increase effectiveness of supply chain?				
7. Avoid potential additional costs (cost avoidance) ?				
8. Reduce current cost basis and improve cost efficiency (cost reduction)?				
9. Improve business knowledge?				
10. Increase research productivity?				

Fig. 5.8 Assessing strategic alignment of proposed investment

- Does the project support company growth in terms of
  - Adding a new business?
  - Increasing customer value?
  - Increasing existing customer binding?
  - Increasing production flexibility?
  - Creating a unique and sustainable advantage?
- Does the project enable cost effectiveness in terms of
  - Increasing the effectiveness of the supply chain?
  - Avoiding potential additional costs?
  - Reducing the current cost base, improve cost efficiency?
  - Improving business knowledge?
  - Increasing research productivity?

Each of the ten CSFs can be assessed with values, for instance "high" (4 points), "medium" (2 points) or "low" (1 point).

Based on the financial analysis and the CSFs assessment, it is possible to define the value contribution and the strategic alignment of each project proposed.

The assessment of the CSFs for a proposed investment is of course subjective. Nevertheless, it is interesting to ask different persons from the same company to make the assessment on their own. It is sometimes amazing to notice that the different assessments may converge. In this case, the employees have a common understanding of the relevant investments.

Once the assessments are available, a positioning matrix can be defined as shown on Fig. 5.9:

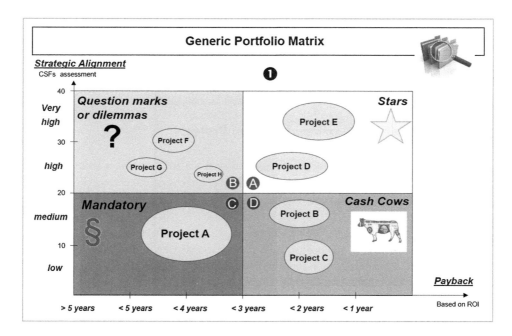

Fig. 5.9 Positioning of projects in the portfolio matrix

Based on the portfolio matrix, a differentiation can be made depending on the Return-on-Investment and the strategic alignment:

- **Stars** provide a high value contribution and a high strategic alignment. They combine current benefit potential with future possible profits
- **Question Marks** provide a strong support to the strategic alignment but have a low value contribution. They should be carefully managed with high management attention, as they may be an important source for future profits
- **Cash Cows** present a strong value contribution but a low strategic alignment
- **Dogs** or **Mandatory projects** must be conducted most of the time even if the corresponding investments do not contribute to the development of the company

The ranking scale for the project portfolio might base on following rules:

1. high value contribution: less than 3 years payback (counted from project start)
2. high strategic alignment: >20 points according to the CSFs assessment

The experience shows that a project portfolio should be balanced. This means especially that it is necessary to invest in question marks in order to get the stars. In avoidance of risks, one can conduct some piloting activities or "trial balloons" with "throw-away" solutions to win valuable experience.

Exercises

Identify the different projects in your company:

- Stars: ………..
- Question marks: ……..
- Cash cows: ………….
- Mandatory: …………

5.2.4   Step 3: Setup, Launch and Monitor Projects

It is important to properly define the interactions between portfolio and project management when launching the project, during its conduction and at the end of the project (Fig. 5.10).

Before launching a project, a name must be chosen. Some central elements must be fixed, like milestone deadlines or the project organisation. A risk profile needs to be determined and a budget line is agreed upon.

During the conduction of the project, a status report must be delivered by the project leader to the portfolio manager on a monthly or at least quarterly basis.

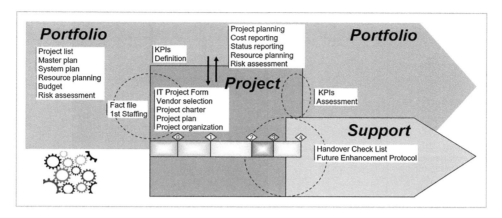

Fig. 5.10 Interactions between portfolio and project

At the end of the project, the handover to the support organisation is key. In case all requirements could not be implemented during the project, enhancements can be identified and should be developed in the future.

To track the fulfilment of the project requirements, specific key-performance indicators (KPIs) can be defined at the beginning of a major project. The KPIs mentioned are based on:

- Scope & deliverables
- Budget
- Time
- Business satisfaction
- Knowledge sharing

Each item is given a weight. The total of points for the project assessment can be for instance 100 points.

These KPIs are defined before the end of "milestone one" and are assessed at the end of the project.

When more than two projects are closely dependent, it is recommended to set-up a so-called "programme". The aim of the programme is to guarantee the success of overall objectives, and not only project-specific aims. The programme duration starts from the kick-off of the first project until the end of the last project. Ideally, a programme is conducted by a programme management team of two to three persons: a business programme manager, an IT programme manager and a coordination programme manager (an external person can be chosen for this role) (Fig. 5.11).

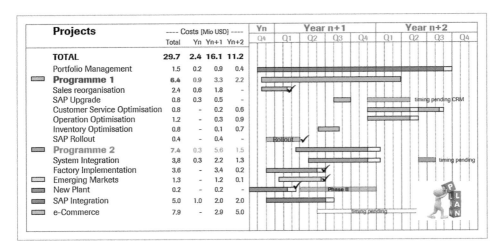

Fig. 5.11 Keeping the overview by means of a portfolio

5.2.5   Step 4: Evaluate Achievements

It is important to evaluate achievements once the project is ended.

A major difficulty to check if a business case has been realised or not, is the fact that this can only be done 2 or 3 years after the project is finalised. The missing causality between company performance and the project achieved remains one of the main challenges. Nevertheless, it is worth trying to track benefits.

The aim of the benefit tracking is:

- To identify tangible benefits based on the business case information provided
- To assess non tangible benefits based on the cost avoidance analysis
- To proof strategic alignment
- To provide management with the indicators needed to manage the business
- To enable project planning and control
- To reinforce worthwhile change and build a momentum for further change
- To demonstrate to the company the value for investment

The benefit tracking roots in the definition of the Business KPIs. These should already be identified in the project business case, so at the very beginning. Or at least, one aim should be to oblige the business to measure its performance KPIs once IT projects are implemented.

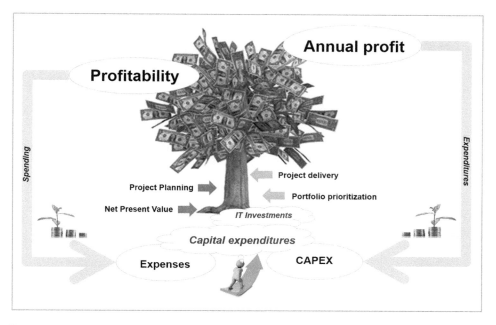

Fig. 5.12   Ecosystem of IT investments

The benefit tracking activities should be under the responsibility of the controlling unit for a corresponding business area. Adjusted objectives may be introduced in the corresponding yearly budget baselines (Fig. 5.12).

5.2.6   IT Project Portfolio Lifecycle

The following picture gives an overview of the interactions between the different management layers of an organisation (Fig. 5.13).

Conflict potential between the portfolio manager and project leaders may appear and it is useful to define "rules" or so-called "powers reserved". An escalation is always possible but should be used as a last resort.

Table 5.2 lists areas where some bottlenecks or even conflicts may appear.

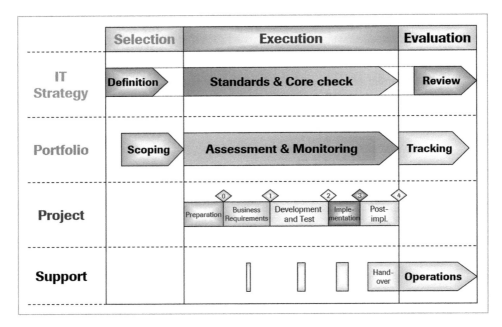

Fig. 5.13 Aligning strategy, portfolio, projects and support

Table 5.2 Possible sources of conflicts between a portfolio manager and project leaders

Topic	Role of the portfolio manager	Role of the project leader
Project time scheduling	• Projects time schedules harmonisation • Decision making in case of conflicts • Synchronisation of milestones and go-live deadlines	• Working out project time schedules
Project deliverables	• Definition of standard deliverables • Coordination of project specific deliverable adjustment • Deliverable review • Definition of development and test strategies • Working out inter-project synergies	• Proposal of project specific deliverable requirements • Working out deliverables
Costs & benefits	• Review of budget requirements and estimated benefits • Decision preparation for management board • Cost and benefit tracking • Summarisation of controlling figures, • Responsibility for reaching the overall portfolio's cost and benefit approach	• Definition of required budgets out of the project plan • Definition and communication of estimated benefits • Project management based on agreed costs and benefits. • Responsibility for reaching the project's cost and benefit approach

5.3   IT Project Management

A project is a planned piece of work to achieve specific purposes in a limited timeframe. Projects are complex, require resources, involve different organisational units and have a defined timescale.

With an increasing number of projects, an organization will identify that life becomes easier if projects are managed in a standardised way, following a common methodology either taken out of literature or developed autonomously. Within this sub-chapter, a project management methodology is presented that is based on best practice and experience.

The objectives of the project management methodology are to define

- practical
- workable
- liveable

guidelines to ensure the successful delivery of projects – permanently.

The main drivers are (Fig. 5.14):

- To define roles and responsibility during the project and after go-live
- To set clear deliverables
- To plan activities and reporting processes to manage external and internal resources
- To achieve quality standards for the optimisation of business processes and system maintenance
- To use a standardised approach to conduct projects on time, within budget and with the required level of quality

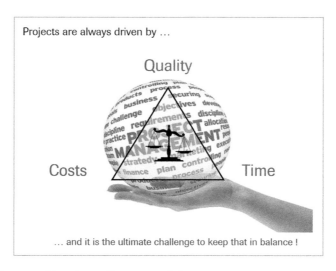

Fig. 5.14 Projects are driven by quality, cost, and time

The structure of the proposed project management methodology is as follows:

- **Introduction**
  To define the purpose and scope of the guidelines
- **Project organisation**
  To provide the structure, roles and responsibilities within a project
- **Project phases**
  To provide procedures to deliver in time
- **Project support processes**
  To provide rules and advice about important project support processes for the success-ful implementation of a project

5.3.1 Introducing the Project Management

The project management is the art to conduct projects (Fig. 5.15).

As already mentioned, projects are limited in time with a start and an end. In order to manage what happens in between, it is recommended to define four key elements which enable the project leader to conduct the project. These elements are (Figs. 5.16, 5.17, 5.18, and 5.19):

- **Phase**
  A project phase is a bundle of project activities, with a start and an end date.
  The end of each phase is defined as a milestone. The steering committee is responsible for the validation of each milestone and should take the "continue" call for the next phase.
- **Milestone**
  Each project phase ends with a milestone which indicates that a significant stage of the project has been reached.

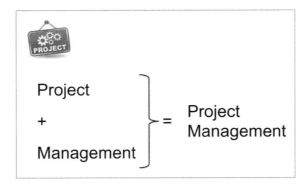

Fig. 5.15 What is project management?

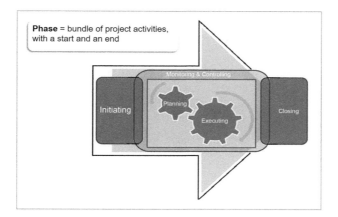

Fig. 5.16 Definition of a project phase

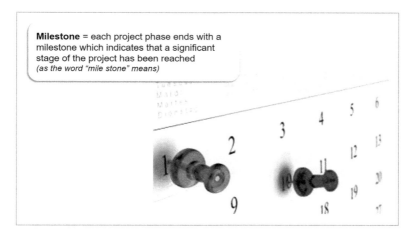

Fig. 5.17 Definition of a milestone

- **Quality gate**
  The quality gate determines whether the project has achieved the exit criteria or not. This is defined by means of determining whether the milestone has been reached or not, and if the results are satisfactory or not.
  Should a quality gate be "red" – this does not mean automatically that the project should be stopped – a review of the risk matrix is recommended and a critical assessment of the project plan may be needed.
- **Deliverable**
  Deliverables are tangible or intangible objects produced as a result of the project that is intended to be delivered to a customer (either internal or external). A deliverable could be a report, a document, a work package, a server upgrade or any other building block of the project.

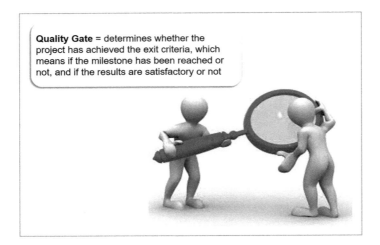

Fig. 5.18 Definition of a project quality gate

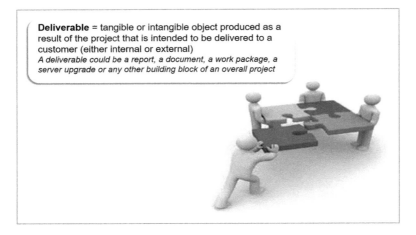

Fig. 5.19 Definition of a project deliverable

At the end of each phase, a decision needs to be taken: the quality gate is exactly the point between two project phases to decide if the next phase can be started or not.

The decision should be based on following considerations:

1. "*Continue*": All activities have been achieved according to the project plan so that the phase can be closed and the project can continue as scheduled.
2. "*Rework*": If some activities show significant discrepancies in relevant areas (cost, time, scope), it can be decided to rebuild them in order to close the phase.
3. "*Stop*": Events occurred that make the project continuation impossible. The project will be stopped and if necessary completely closed. Respectively, some conditions need to be changed.

5.3.2   Project Organisation

In order to successfully conduct a project, a dedicated organisation needs to be defined, where roles and project members are clearly visualised.

The Fig. 5.20 shows a generic project organisation. However, for each project a specific project organigram needs to be defined.

The following key functions should be defined in order to set up a project organigram. The functions needed depend on the project size or complexity:

- Project sponsor
- Steering committee
- Project leader and deputy
- Work stream leader
- Project member
- Project management office (optional)
- Project quality office (optional)

The same person may fulfil different roles in the project organisation. Nevertheless, a situation should be avoided in which the project manager is the only person working on the project.

There are various ways to define the structure of sub-project levels. This should be considered when setting up the organigram. Sub-projects can be organised for instance according to the company's organisational structure, project phases or project activities.

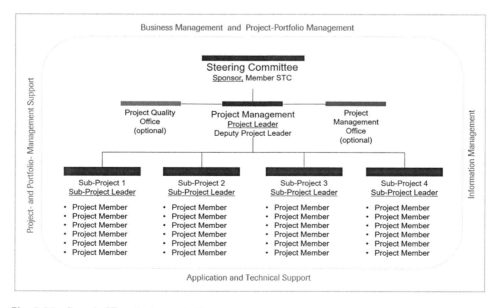

Fig. 5.20   Generic IT project organisation

5.3.2.1 Project Sponsor

The project sponsor takes ownership of the project and promotes it throughout the business. This person may take responsibility over the followings tasks:

Project commitment
- Fosters the management of change by ensuring that no operational or organisational barriers hinder the project
- Takes ownership of the project budget and approves any variations in expenditures from budget and assists with resolving expenditure problems
- Monitors project costs and assures adherence to budget
- Ensures delivery of the benefits in accordance with the business case
- Serves as chair of the steering committee
- Liaises with other project sponsors and line management to resolve conflicts, for instance over resource allocation

Project definition
- Defines the scope and the objectives of the project in accordance with business goals
- Ensures that the project supports the achievement of the business objectives

Project approval
- Is able to present the project to the appropriate management and review boards for approval to achieve endorsement and commitment of resources
- Obtains agreement on the definition of the project and approves progress and results at key milestones during the project

Project authority
- Delegates authority to the project leader for the execution of the project
- Ensures that resource issues constraining the project are resolved and if outside his/her control seeks the support of senior management or the appropriate review board

Project review
- Should be informed about the project progress and delivery
- Deals with significant management issues and initiates corrective actions if needed
- Ensures that milestones, changes to scope, plans, budgets and quality are agreed and processed properly

Appraisals
- Can define an appraisal mechanism at the beginning of the project for project members, especially for the project manager
- Can assess the final quality of the project implementation
- Gives appraisals according to defined goals of the yearly employees' objectives

5.3.2.2 Steering Committee (STC)

Members of the steering committee should be made up of representatives of the business areas, line managers and members of the board involved in or affected by the implementation of the project.

Following tasks need to be taken into account by the STC members:

Authority	• Monitor and control project progress (financial, time, scope and quality) including "continue" decisions at the end of a milestone
	• Seek approval from business management where costs are expected to exceed the agreed budget or the benefits expected are likely to be less than anticipated
Further responsibilities	• Seek approval for resources
	• Report progress and exceptions to business management
	• Obtain approval of corrective actions as required and initiated by the project leader
	• Provide recommendations for resolving scope related matters
	• Serve as liaison between the project manager and the senior management
	• Take decisions on business topics needed for the conduction of the project

5.3.2.3 Project Leader

The project leader is appointed by the project sponsor and is responsible for the successful implementation of the project, especially regarding budget, resources, schedules, scope and quality, compliance and risks. This person may delegate tasks but retains responsibility. As the project leader is a key person for a project, this person should be an internal employee.

Also, a deputy should be nominated. This is especially recommended for critical projects with a longer duration. Together with the work stream leaders the project leader builds the project team.

The project leader must fulfil following activities:

Project management	• Manages, monitors, controls and completes project activities in accordance to agreed plans and budget
	• Resolves all issues affecting project execution, with the assistance of the project sponsor and project steering committee as required
	• Prepares, presents and reviews the project charter
	• Reviews and approves project deliverables
	• Reports progress and raises issues with the project sponsor and the steering committee
	• Manages project resources
	• Identifies, prioritises, plans, and assigns the project tasks
	• Manages costs, benefits and risks
	• Sets up project organisation and manages the project team
	• Assists the project sponsor in ensuring that the business benefits are delivered as expected
	• Escalates issues to the steering committee or to the sponsor
Quality management	• Assures compliance with project management guidelines and system delivery
	• Ensures that the quality assurance and compliance activities are carried out and documented properly
	• Ensures that projects deliver functionality and quality on time and enable benefits
	• Ensures compliance to policies
Relationship management	• Coordinates with all other projects and line functions that affect or are affected by the assigned project, including legal office, procurement etc
Status reporting	• Reports project progress (especially potential delays or budget overrun)
	• Reviews progress against the plan baseline

5.3.2.4 Work Stream Leader

The work stream leader is responsible for contributing to overall project objectives and specific team deliverables. This person is leading a work stream team and must fulfil following tasks:

Project management	• Prepares, presents and reviews the detailed sub-project plan
	• Manages, monitors, controls and completes activities and tasks in accordance to the project plan
	• Resolves all issues affecting project execution, with the assistance of the experts and key users as required
	• Reports progress and raises issues to the project leader
	• Escalate issues to the project leader
Coordination	• Coordinates and organises jointly with the other team leaders common project activities, like for instance integration tests, cutover activities and end-user training
	• Establishes effective communication channels within the project team

5.3.2.5 Project Members

The project members include all resources necessary to execute the project. The project staff has complementary skills and works actively on the project. Each member reports to a work stream leader. The following are major tasks:

Project task execution	• Contribute to the overall project objectives and specific team deliverables
	• Provide expertise in various processes
	• Work with users to ensure the project meets business needs
	• Escalate issues to the work stream leader
	• Analyse and document current and future processes/systems

5.3.2.6 Project Management Office (Optional)

If the project manager cannot embrace all project management activities, a project management office (PMO) may be set up. The PMO activities may depend on the needs and the nature of the project. The activities mentioned below are "typical" PMO tasks:

Controlling	• Orders a project number
	• Performs monthly project budget and cost controlling
	• Periodically checks appropriate cost allocation to corresponding project number

Administrative support	• Provides support to the project management regarding office infrastructure, staff administration and access rights, steering committee presentation, status reporting etc
	• Monitors time recording, supports cost controlling and invoices verification
	• Manages project documentation
	• Collects paper documentation
Communication	• Provides internal communication activities, e.g. info-, kick-off meeting, project presentations, team building activities and social events
	• Provides external communication activities, e.g. logo, newsletter, web page and demos

5.3.2.7 Project Quality Office (Optional)

Optionally, a project quality office can be set up. This is normally recommended for bigger projects. The team of the project quality office may consist of internal and/or external members. Quality management ensures that the project will satisfy its objectives and requirements.

Quality assurance	• Ensures compliance with the current project management methodology
	• Performs project audits and provides written reports
	• Performs final quality checks during the handover from the project team to the support units
	• Archives all project-related papers and electronic documents, like project charter, project plan, contracts, time sheets, invoices, status/audit reports and handover protocols
Compliance	• Performs compliance checks
	• Writes a validation plan at the beginning of a project
	• Conducts validation audits and provides a written report to the project leader, the sponsor and the steering committee members
	• Provides a validation report to the project leader, the sponsor and the steering committee members and gives the final agreement for going-live

5.3.3   Project Phases

In order to meet project objectives, it is judicious to define phases and to process them step by step. It is also important to ensure that the deliverables produced in each phase meet their purpose, and that project team members are properly prepared for the next phase.

For each phase a Work Breakdown Structure (WBS) should be defined, where the different tasks and deliverables are identified. At the end of each phase, the steering committee signs off on the achievements and quality of the main deliverables.

The project phases may differ depending on the nature of the project. For a small project, three phases may be sufficient whereas many more phases are needed for a longer rollout project. In general, it is necessary to include a definition phase at the beginning of a project in order to define the project and to inform all impacted organisational units.

The proposed project management methodology embraces five main phases in order to have an overall framework. The Fig. 5.21 gives an overview on the five phases and their main deliverables:

Phase 1: **Preparation**
This phase deals with the preparation of the project, especially the definition of the project objectives and their business relevance, the project organisation, the resources needed, the project planning including the project activities that need to be achieved.
Phase 2: **Blueprint**
This phase aims at defining the business requirements, process specifications and the project deliverables.
Phase 3: **Development & Test**
This phase corresponds to the development of the system. It must be guaranteed that quality and compliance requirements are fulfilled.

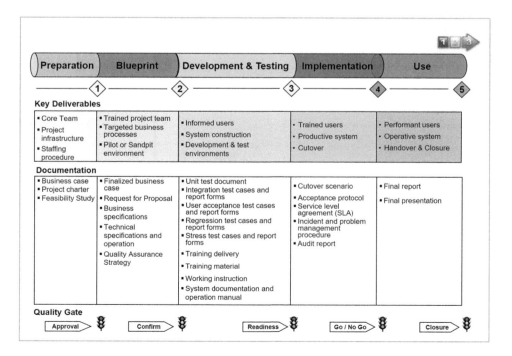

Fig. 5.21 Generic IT project phases

Phase 4: **Implementation**

Before the new system is used, some cutover activities have to be conducted to switch to a productive mode. Above all user training, operating procedures and cutover activities.

Phase 5: **Use**

This final phase deals with the efficient use of the new system. The transition must be clearly defined including post implementation support. The closure of the project remains the last activity to be accomplished.

5.3.3.1 Delivery Strategy

In order to ensure the success of a project, it is necessary to define which steps are necessary to make sure that all conditions are fulfilled to achieve the set objectives. In this course each project is split in several phases. The phases intimately depend on the nature and the aims of the project. The so-called "delivery strategy" is the basis to have appropriate phases in place, where the phased approach to deliver the expected results is designed.

For the art of organising an efficient project delivery, several approaches have been defined, as one can find by looking at the project management literature.

In the IT area, following approaches are worth to be mentioned (Source: Wikipedia):

- *Waterfall*: a sequential design process, in which progress is seen as flowing steadily downwards (like a waterfall) through the phases of conception, initiation, analysis, design, construction, testing, production/implementation and maintenance.
- *V-Model*: graphical representation of the system's development lifecycle, summarising the main steps to be taken in conjunction with the corresponding deliverables within the IT development framework.
- *Agile*: solutions evolve through collaboration between self-organising, cross-functional teams, promoting adaptive planning, evolutionary development, early delivery, continuous improvement. This encourages rapid and flexible responses to change.
- *Scrum*: iterative and incremental agile software development methodology for managing product development where "a flexible, holistic product development strategy in which a development team works as a unit to reach a common goal" is defined.

Questions

1. Is Scrum compatible with a phased approach?
2. What is the most effective way to deliver within an IT project?

The sequential approach remains a simple method to plan the different phases and get a first "feeling" about the tasks to be achieved. The planning of the project then follows the sequence of the phases. It is also interesting to perform a "retro-planning". This means to start planning the project from the end, in order to check whether the designed plan is realistic or not and to identify potential bottlenecks.

5.3.3.2 Phase 1: Preparation

The phase "preparation" is the required starting point for all projects (Fig. 5.22). This phase deals with the project planning and initiation activities. Before a project gets started, the approval for the investment should be given.

As usual, it is important to understand the starting position and the objectives to be achieved. As many dependencies may exist, the scope of the project must be carefully analysed and interdependencies need to be identified.

The major activities are:

- Identify a sponsor and nominate the project leader
- Set up the project organisation and select internal project members and external partners
- Design an overall project plan
- Prepare a kick-off meeting
- Perform training for the project team
- Prepare the project infrastructure
- Perform a risk analysis and set up of a risk mitigation plan

At the end of this phase, the STC has to give its approval for the conduction of the project. Depending on the amount of the project costs, an approval from the company board (and possibly from the board of administration) may be required.

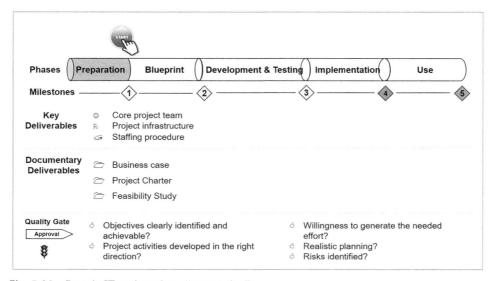

Fig. 5.22 Generic IT project phase "preparation"

STC Check List for "Approval" Decision

Following points need to be clearly defined and reported so that the STC can take a decision:

- **Problem description and definition of the objectives**: Are the problems understood and are the objectives of the project clearly identified and achievable?
- **Changes in process and organisation**: Are the changes in process and organisation adequate and enforceable according to the objectives?
- **Matching between the declared project goal and the business intent**: Are project activities designed accordingly? Where are remaining doubts? Is the overview sufficient (organisational blindness)?
- **Costs, benefit, and profitability**: How high is the willingness to generate the needed effort? Can the benefits be assured? Is the project team really able to make sure that the benefits will be achieved?
- **Business view on deadlines, milestones and deliverables**: Are the milestones and deliverables properly defined? Is the planning realistic?
- **Risks**: Are the main risks already identified?
- **Quality gate "approval":** all stakeholders understand the rationale of the project and agree to launch the next phase of the project

5.3.3.3 Phase 2: Blueprint

The purpose of the phase "Blueprint" is to analyse the system and user requirements and to specify the project deliverables (Fig. 5.23). A possible approach includes the following steps:

- As-is analysis, as a result of workshops with business and IT representatives and visualised with brown papers
- To-be model, documented in whitepapers (process flows) approved by the business process owners
- Gap identification, where the activities needed to further the phase are listed

The major activities are:

- Perform workshops to understand existing business processes
- Document business processes, including any discrepancies with a standard model, that will be implemented and obtain the approval of the business process owners
- Specify the technical features of the system to be implemented, including for data model, data loads, interfaces, programs and authorisations
- If required, perform a product evaluation and selection analysis
- Set up a sandpit environment for an initial assessment of the technical solution
- Perform review of scope, time, costs and benefits to be approved by the steering committee

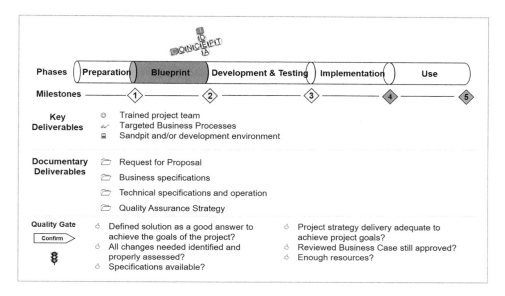

Fig. 5.23   Generic IT project phase "blueprint"

STC Check List for "Confirm" Decision

At the end of the "Blueprint" phase, the STC has to give its agreement for the delivery of the project, according to the following criteria:

- **Solution description**: Does the defined solution provide a good answer to achieve the goals of the project?
- **Changes of processes and organisation**: Have all the changes needed been identified and properly assessed? Are specifications available and approved?
- **Alignment of project goal with business intent**: Is the project strategy delivery adequate to achieve the project goals? Does it match with the business intention?
- **Costs, benefit and profitability**: Is the organisation ready to invest resources in the project? Is the reviewed business case still approved? Is the project team able to realise the benefits? Are there enough resources?
- **Business view of deadlines, milestones and deliverables**: Are the milestones and deliverables measurable and appraisable? Is the planning realistic?
- **Risks and mitigation measures**: Are all potential risks been identified? Are mitigation measures approved and planned?
- **Quality gate "confirm":** after an analysis of the requirements and the resources needed, all stakeholders agree with the delivery strategy, the number and kind of resources needed to achieve the goals. The STC is convinced that the business case is still valid.

5.3.3.4 Phase 3: Development & Test

The purpose of the phase "Development & Test" is to build and extensively test the proposed system according to the business requirements, as defined in the "Blueprint" phase (Fig. 5.24).

The major activities are:

- Develop and customise the development and consolidation systems
- Set up test scenarios and perform tests
- Set up and implement authorisation and security concepts
- Plan of IT architecture and infrastructure
- Develop training concept and plan user training
- Produce user manuals

STC Check List for "Readiness" Decision

The steering committee has to evaluate the quality of the new system that needs to be put in place, according to the following criteria:

- **Acceptance report related to the technical solution, processes and organisation, operation and migration**: Are the acceptance reports related to technical solution, processes and organisation, operation and migration available? Where are the major concerns in terms of quality?
- **Accordance with original and revised objectives**: Is the project on track? Are all system functionalities available according to the defined requirements?

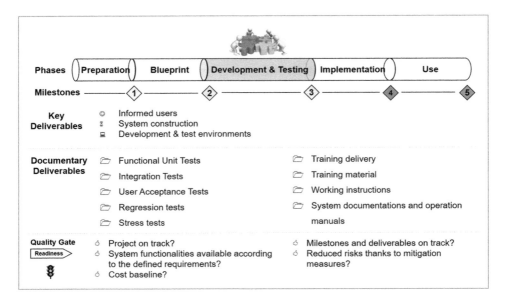

Fig. 5.24 Generic IT project phase "development & testing"

- **Costs, benefit and profitability**: What is the cost baseline? Are the benefits achievable? Can the business case still be performed?
- **Business view of deadlines, milestones and deliverables**: Are the milestones and deliverables on track? Is the planning still achievable?
- **Risks and mitigation measures**: Have identified risks been reduced by means of mitigation measures? Is there an updated list of risks discussed with the persons concerned?
- **Quality gate "readiness":** Does the solution developed meet the defined requirements? Can the quality of the system be guaranteed? Are potential users informed and trained?

5.3.3.5 Phase 4: Implementation

The implementation leads to a productive system, which includes the entire manual and automated procedures, data, trained staff and training material, installed application products and documentation (Fig. 5.25).

The major activities are:

- Perform stress test
- Perform user training
- Set-up technical operations procedures
- Develop a cutover plan
- Set-up problem and change management procedures
- Perform final quality check
- Perform the solution deployment

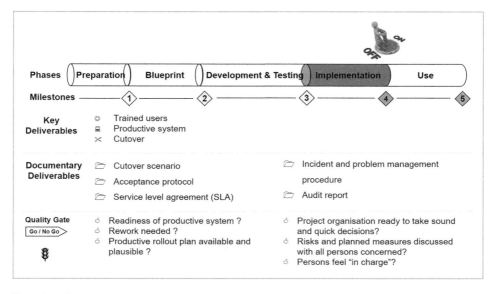

Fig. 5.25 Generic IT project phase "implementation"

STC Check List for "Go/No Go" Decision

The STC has to give its okay to set up the new system productive according to the following criteria:

- **Readiness of productive system (technical solution, process and organisation, operation and migration)**: Are status reports related to the technical solution, processes and organisation, operation and migration of the project implementation available? Is rework needed prior to the productive rollout?
- **Productive rollout plan and procedures**: Is the productive rollout plan available and plausible for all components, (a) technical system, (b) processes and organisation, (c) migration and (d) operation?
- **Fast decision path**: Is the project organisation (or at least part of the operational organisation) ready to take sound and quick decisions?
- **Risks and mitigation measures**: Is there an updated list with risks and planned measures discussed with all persons concerned?
- **Commitment, responsibility and measures to assure benefit**: Who is responsible for making sure that all cutover tasks are coordinated? Are there enough qualified resources? Do the persons feel "in charge"?
- **Quality gate "go/no go"**: does the STC agree to put the system into production? If not, what are the consequences and what is the "plan B"?

5.3.3.6 Phase 5: Use

The go-live is the operational birthday of the new solution. Post-implementation support ensures that the system works properly and that system maintenance is in place (Fig. 5.26).

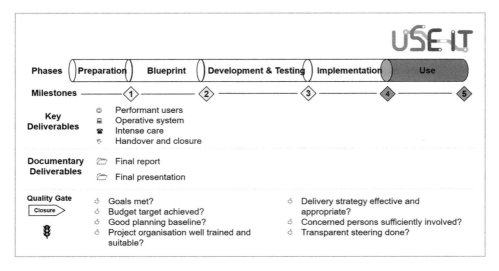

Fig. 5.26 Generic IT project phase "use"

The major activities of this phase are:

- Perform go-live
- Produce post-implementation review
- Define roles and responsibilities with the support units regarding
  - future enhancements
  - future responsibilities
  - contingency planning and risk assessment
- Perform handover activities, including information meetings, training sessions, intense care of the users, and delivery of project and system documentation to the business and the support units

STC Check List for "Closing" Decision
The STC has to agree to close the project according to following criteria:

- **Accordance with original and revised objectives**: Are the goals met? Was the scope still managed in case all objectives could not be realised (descoping, work-arounds …)?
- **Costs, benefit and business case**: Was the budget target achieved? Why and where not?
- **Business view on deadlines, milestones and deliverables**: Were the milestones and deliverables sufficiently good defined and reached? Was there a good planning baseline?
- **Risks and mitigation measures**: Were the risks actively managed and were the mitigation measures suitable? Were many new risks detected during the project?
- **Project organisation**: Was the project organisation well trained and suitable for reaching the goals?
- **Project delivery**: Was the delivery strategy effective and appropriate for reaching the goals?
- **Person involved and concerned**: Were concerned persons sufficiently involved?
- **Planning**: Was the planning appropriate and reliable?
- **Control**: Was a transparent steering performed during the project?
- **Quality assurance**: Were measures taken and implemented in order to ensure the project plan and lead of the project results (review, four-eyes-principle)?
- **Quality gate "closing":** Does the STC agree to close the project? Which activities still need to be addressed and are hand-over sessions planned?

5.3.4   Support Processes

The so-called "support processes" are defined as activities which need to be carried out throughout the whole duration of the project.

The Fig. 5.27 gives an overview of the support processes defined.

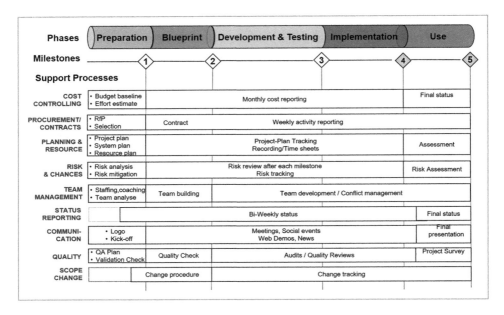

Fig. 5.27 Overview of project management support processes

5.3.4.1 Cost Controlling

The project leader should be able to assess the financial situation at any point of time during the project, especially the project cost estimate, so-called "forecast", compared to the budget baseline.

Project cost controlling deals with primary costs and includes:

Project expenditure:
- Facility
- IT-expenditure
- Communication
- Marketing
- Travel expenses
- Consultancy, revision
- Transaction charges, postage
- Leasing
- Other costs

Investments:
- Real estate
- Renovation own estate
- Renovation external estate
- Machines
- Furniture
- Software
- Hardware

Project expenditure are considered to be "operational" costs for the project whereas investment amounts are amortised depending on the nature of the asset.

In order to track the budget baseline, it is recommended to create a line per type of costs and per supplier over the duration of the project. A monthly tracking of the project costs should be planned by including the corresponding amounts once invoices are received (Fig. 5.28).

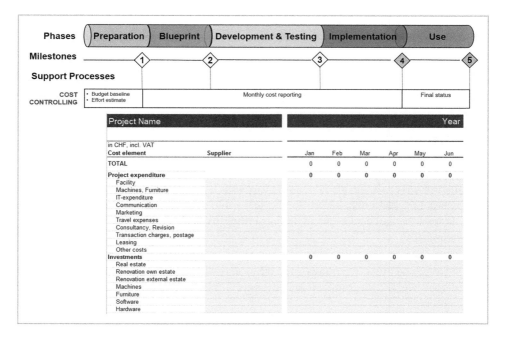

Fig. 5.28 Managing a project budget

5.3.4.2 Procurement & Contracts

When implementing new infrastructure, tools, automated solutions or services, it is important to select appropriate providers with the necessary knowledge. Corresponding selection activities are part of the project and need to be planned. A proper supplier selection increases the chance of success and also enables to achieve investments, which are in line with the market.

For major projects, it is necessary to ask at least three suppliers in order to guarantee the clause of non-preference. Different criteria can be used to assess the potential performance of a supplier, for instance:

- business functionalities (fulfilment, ergonomics)
- technical evaluation (architecture, standards & openness, application lifecycle, performance/scalability)
- vendor profile (company, market & partnership strategy, product strategy, local representation, references and contacts)

Once the selection of the provider is closed, it is necessary to get a signed agreement. For major contracts, a review from the legal department is needed.

Depending on the nature of the products or services delivered, it is important to check the quality of the service delivery. For instance by assessing the relevance of a consultancy post-interim.

5.3.4.3 Planning & Resources

The management of time and allocated resources is essential for project management. Furthermore, the project manager must make sure that the people involved in the project are trained, motivated and confident about the project schedules over the whole duration of the project.

In order to have a realistic planning, the three following steps are highly recommended:

- **Before project start**
  It is important to have an estimate of the required effort. Therefore, the project manager should have frequent discussions with the respective involved entities.
  Estimation methods can also be used, especially:
  1. Manpower planning: based on the tasks and on the subsequent work-packages planned, resources are calculated according to the skills needed and to the effort estimated.
  2. Process based effort estimation: based on the number of business process flows and the assigned "function points", the effort in time and person-days is estimated. This method needs data from completed projects. The more data, the more valuable the estimation.
- **During the project**
  It is vital to make sure that the team members have understood their roles, that they have the proper competencies and that they feel motivated and confident to deliver results according to the project plan.
- **At the end of the project**
  The project manager has to make sure that all activities are executed in order to ensure a successful end of the project.

It is important for the project manager to know where bottlenecks are. To do so, it is vital to identify the so-called critical path. If one activity on the critical path has a delay, the whole project is impacted. A project delay may also have an impact on other projects if interdependencies apply.

The project plan also represents the basis for scheduling project activities. It is recommended to have a metric in place to measure the progress of the project. For instance, the number of documents to be migrated can be measured or the number of tests conducted.

The time frame of the project plan should be in accordance with the degree of detail of the project activities. It is of no benefit to plan a whole project lasting more than 1 year in daily time intervals. Therefore, a distinction between a "high level" and a "detailed" planning is made (Fig. 5.29).

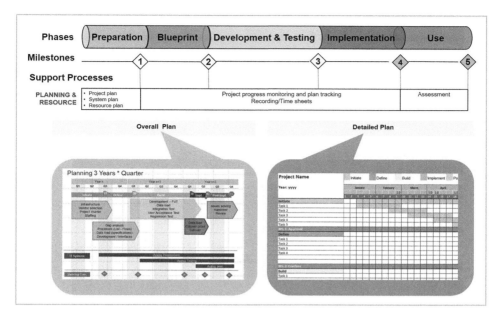

Fig. 5.29 Planning time, systems and resources

5.3.4.4 Risks & Chances

Risks are common factors in every project that need to be identified and tracked. Assessment and mitigation are key-responsibilities of a project management. The following section describes the methods and tools to manage risks within a project.

A risk is based on the "feeling" that something can go wrong and will then have a very negative effect on the success of the project. Therefore, it is important to be aware of the potential threats from the very beginning of the project.

Following steps are needed to manage risks within a project:

- **Step 1: identify the risks**
  Only those who are sufficiently aware of risks will be in a position to manage these risks. The initial identification of risks can be carried out during the project kick-off.
- **Step 2: assess the risk**
  The risk needs to be assessed as a product of the potential loss and the probability of occurrence. The impact is assessed on a scale from (1) low to (4) redhibitory, whereas the likelihood is measured on a graduation between (1) improbable and (5) certain.
- **Step 3: draw the risk matrix**
  The risk matrix includes a risk categorisation, the risk description, the potential loss and the probability of occurrence. It enables to visualise the different risks of the project and gives a first idea of the criticality concerning the chances of success.

- **Step 4: draft measures to mitigate risks**
  Especially for the "critical" risks, measures need to be defined either to avoid the risk or to lower the impact of it.
- **Step 5: decide on risk mitigation measures**
  Mitigation activities may require resources and must be agreed by the STC, which may also decide to take the risks into account without having any mitigation in place.
- **Step 6: mitigate identified risks**
  Based on the agreed mitigation activities, these need to be implemented by the project manager.
- **Step 7: review risk assessment and check the effect of mitigation activities**
  Risks and conducted mitigation activities need to be assessed and reviewed on a regular basis. Especially at the end of each phase, it is highly recommended to draw the new risk matrix and to indicate the evolution of each single risk.

It is also important that the project management is aware of chances, for instance by rallying support, identifying synergies or promoting new employees (Fig. 5.30).

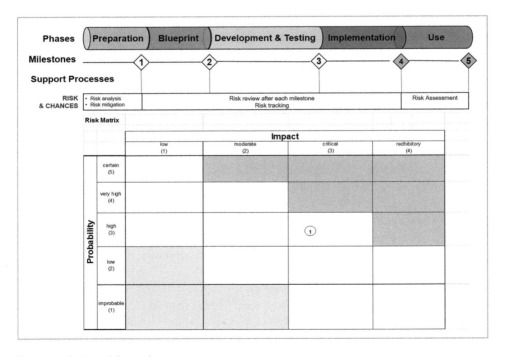

Fig. 5.30 Project risk matrix

5.3.4.5 Team Management

People management and team building are essential for each project phase. When handling critical phases of a project, it is important to dispose of tools and methods to deal with possible conflicts and human problems.

In order to have good team work and to minimise the complexity of projects, it is helpful to have the tools and methods in place such as:

- **Team Management System (TMS)**
  This system helps team members to understand how they can work together to produce high team performance. The TMS is an analysis tool which offers personalised feedback on the preferred way in which a person or a team works in four key areas:
  - Relationship with others
  - Decision making
  - Gathering and using information
  - Organisation of self and others
- **Project navigation**
  Objectives achievable with project navigation are:
  - Optimised quality and reduced time in project realisation
  - Increased efficiency of resources
  - Better use of talents and skills of all members
  - Less dependency on a single person
  - Improved quality of decisions
  - Interactive cooperation of team members
  - Higher probability of project success

5.3.4.6 Status Reporting

Status reporting provides an overview on the activities of the project. It also highlights problems and issues that require management attention (Fig. 5.31).

The reporting concerning the current status of the project comprises an assessment concerning the financial situation, the adherence to the plan and to the scope. In general, colours are used to report the status of a project at management level:

- **G (green)** = project parameters are in line with objectives, milestones, budget and scope
- **Y (yellow)** = some parameters do not achieve the objectives totally
- **R (red)** = two or more parameters do not reach the minimum level of quality

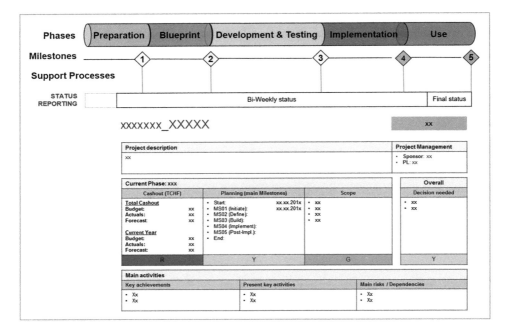

Fig. 5.31 Project status reporting

An overall status is given in addition for each project. In general, the final status is defined by the more critical colour appearing in one of the three topics reported (in terms of worst case scenario). If a project has a yellow overall status, the project manager in cooperation with the sponsor should recommend actions (like budget increase, milestone postponement, descoping, re-priorisation) to be taken so that the overall status gets back into the "green" area. Should a project be reported as red, it is then urgent to organise a STC meeting to analyse the situation and also check a potential impact on the project portfolio (for instance a project postponement impacting other projects).

The status report is a task taken up by the project leader and is sent to the sponsor, steering committee members and the portfolio manager. A summary may be sent to the corporate management board.

5.3.4.7 Communication

Communication is an essential part of a project, as resource and activities need to be coordinated and information exchanged.

It is possible to distinguish between the internal project communication, which concerns the project team and the steering committee, the external project communication which is directed towards the community of users and the external communication which is directed to the customers.

The internal project communication includes:

- Info meetings before project start
- Kick-off meeting with all project members, the project sponsor(s) and possibly the future support team
- Regular project meetings (for instance, every 2 weeks)
- Regular reporting of activities
- Presentations to project sponsor at the end of a milestone
- Steering committee meetings
- Team building activities if needed (especially for longer projects with an heterogeneous group),
- Social events
- Closure meeting to summarise project accomplishments, performance (money, time, and quality) and lessons learned

External project communication deals with:

- Developing a project logo
- Articles in existing or dedicated project newsletters
- Intranet
- Informational e-mails
- Demonstrations and information forums
- Marketing activities (like give-aways)

External communication deals with:

- Mailings
- Publications in news papers
- Internet
- Webpage
- Project events (road-shows…)

5.3.4.8 Quality

Quality is defined as meeting the business requirements. It can also include system interactivity and reliability, process performance and time needed to learn the system.

Project quality is most of the time measured through costs, deadlines, system performance and scope fulfilment.

Audits and checks are required to verify the project quality. This can be done on an ongoing basis or at the end of the project, for instance during the handover.

Lessons learned are very useful and should be organised by the project leader. Feedbacks from business users are also useful to measure customer satisfaction.

5.3.4.9 Scope Changes

Scope changes performed during the project should be traceable. This applies particularly to technical developments on existing IT systems.

It is important to recognise the changes performed at the business process level and the potential impacts on technical links. Changes need to be analysed and the gaps between the current scenario and the recommended solution clearly identified.

To ensure the successful realisation of the project, it is important to track changes and their business relevance.

5.4   The Human Factor

This is the point about project management: motivation has to be regarded as the key to success. It is also important to know and understand the motivation of the team members. If only the project management team is excited about the project, then the performance of the whole team may be insufficient (Fig. 5.32).

It has been noticed that several phases in the behaviour of team members may appear.

1. **Phase 1: Optimism**
   At the beginning the mood of the team members is usually positive. People are curious about the project and the project team is somehow impatient to start.
2. **Phase 2: Reality Shock**
   This phase, in which the team should already bring results, is characterised by uncertainty. Pressure is palpable and tensions appear among the project team. The impact of the project, like staff reduction or budget cuts, may appear clearly and reactions can be perceived and detected.
3. **Success: Winning Spirit**
   First successes may have been achieved and it is highly recommended to celebrate these!

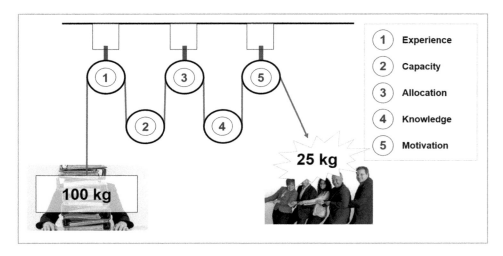

Fig. 5.32 Motivational factors

Thanks to active change management during the project, the "valley of tears" is less deep and can be crossed more quickly (Fig. 5.33).

Certain factors may explain why optimal conditions do not exist at the start of a project, for instance when (Fig. 5.34):

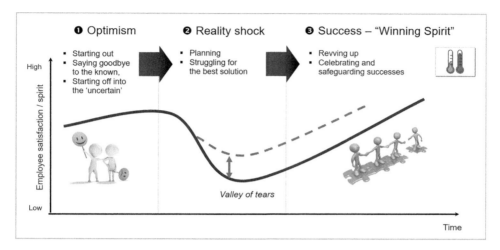

Fig. 5.33 Emotional project curve

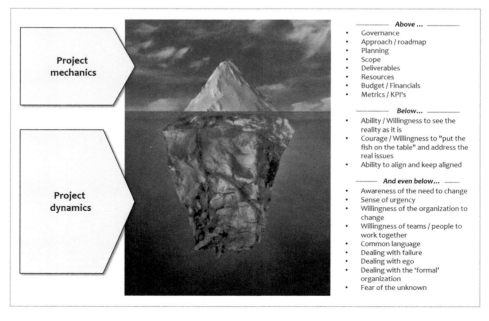

Fig. 5.34 Visible and invisible project risks

- the scope is not clear
- dealing with complexity is postponed to later
- people are not clear about their role and/or responsibilities
- people do not want to work together
- the project requires an alignment between several areas within the organisation
- there is limited visibility on the next steps
- there is no "early wins" looming in the near future

Depending on the way the project is conducted, people will inevitably ask themselves questions in terms of (Fig. 5.35):

- reward and salary
- career development
- job characteristics
- social environment

Experience shows that some simple ingredients are needed to increase the chance of success of a project.

The kick-off meeting remains the starting point, where, in general, the project team meets for the first time (Fig. 5.36). It is essential to make sure that the project members understand the goal to be achieved, the "dangers" to be faced during the trip. The appraisal at the end for the performance should be also communicated. The main task of the project leader is to make sure that all questions are answered so that team members can perform as expected. This includes a good infrastructure, a short decision path, an efficient communication and an inspiring work atmosphere.

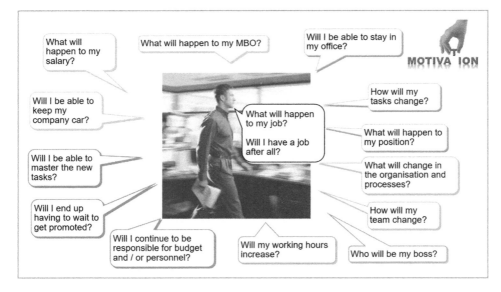

Fig. 5.35 Common questions when changes occur

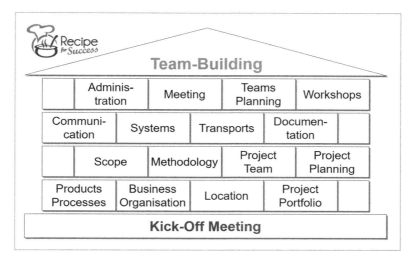

Fig. 5.36 Magic recipe for project management

Learning from past experience is also a good approach to start new projects (Fig. 5.37). It is important to reflect what happened in order to improve future implementations. This task does not take much effort and is very rewarding. The results and findings of the project review can be shared between the stakeholders and documented. By doing this, future project leaders can profit from the experience to valid effort estimates. It can almost be seen as a "ritual" when closing projects and becomes an element of the company's culture.

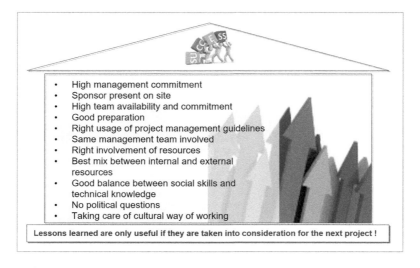

Fig. 5.37 Own learnings from past IT projects

Fig. 5.38 Harvest the fruits of successful projects

The issue concerning project management for a company is not only to conduct a project successfully (Fig. 5.38). The real challenge is to create a culture in which the whole organisation can learn from projects, the so-called "learning organisation". A project team with the corresponding "fighting spirit" will keep this spirit long after the project is delivered. This ability is very valuable to encourage and support continuous employee learning, to spread new knowledge throughout the organisation and to remove traditional hierarchical barriers.

This chapter's last word is formulated by Joy Gumz:

Operations keeps the lights on, strategy provides a light at the end of the tunnel, but project management is the train engine that moves the organization forward.

IT Reporting

6

Abstract

There are many projects and services running in parallel within the IT organization. In addition, activities such as audits, benchmarks or risk assessments are also conducted.

In such a complex environment, it is challenging to keep track of the big picture. However, transparency is of the essence. Key is the organization's ability to capitalize on past experience as opposed to operating in an ad-hoc modus. IT reporting provides an excellent opportunity to keep an overview over activities and thus enables control and guidance.

An abundance of performance reporting models is available and can be successfully combined with the definition of IT processes to design a reporting structure.

Two approaches are presented and tested: bottom-up versus top-down. This chapter helps you to find out, which approach is best suited to have an effective IT reporting in place.

6.1 Introduction

The measure of the performance is one of the trickiest questions for the top management (Fig. 6.1). It requires constant efforts on the one hand and may lead to a technocratic leadership culture, if not carried out properly. On the other hand, having no indicators in place means that you are in a blind flight. So the relevance and the quality (and not just the quantity) of performance indicators are of critical importance. In this context, so-called KPIs, **Key Performance Indicators**, are helpful.

© Springer Fachmedien Wiesbaden GmbH, part of Springer Nature 2018
L. Pilorget, T. Schell, *IT Management*,
https://doi.org/10.1007/978-3-658-19309-6_6

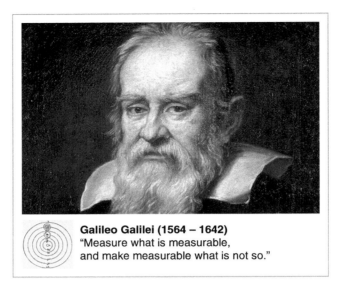

Galileo Galilei (1564 – 1642)
"Measure what is measurable,
and make measurable what is not so."

Fig. 6.1 Making performance measurable

KPIs are measurable values that indicate how effectively an organisation achieves its objectives.

KPIs can be used at all levels of a company: sales (growth of sales revenue), marketing (number of new customers and turnover generated with new contracts), finance (investment return), innovation (number of patents and new products) and many more.

They also apply to processes. Thanks to the formalisation of the process steps, different stages of measurement can be identified: before, between, during, and after the execution of a single process step. Below some generic examples are listed, based on capacity, quality and productivity:

- Average time to complete task
- Overdue time
- Number of errors
- Volume of tasks per staff
- Time allocated for administration, management or training
- Average cycle time from request to delivery
- Customer ratings of service (customer satisfaction)
- Number of customer complaints
- Average time lag between identification of external compliance issues and resolution
- Reduced costs due to stopped or inefficient processes

Questions
1. What can be measured easily?
2. What is difficult or impossible to measure?
3. How is IT performance measured in your organisation?

The current section aims at:

- defining measurable and relevant process KPIs
- knowing the principles of Balanced Scorecard (BSC) and the ability to apply BSC to an IT organisation
- being able to report relevant KPIs to the IT management
- understanding the concept of performance measurement
- gathering knowledge about IT controlling
- understanding the importance and relevance of the budget process

6.2   Performance Measurement

Many models have been developed to enable performance management, especially:

1. Balanced Scorecard (BSC)
2. European Foundation for Quality Management (EFQM)
3. Dashboards
4. Risk-oriented performance management systems

In 1992, Kaplan and David P. Norton (Kaplan/Norton "The balanced scorecard: translating strategy into action" 1996) designed a performance measurement model including a mix of financial and non-financial measures: **the Balanced Scorecard (BSC)** model (Fig. 6.2). Its success was immediate and the scope of application of the framework was rapidly growing.

The model includes four different views for defining and monitoring activities to achieve the strategic intent of the organisation.

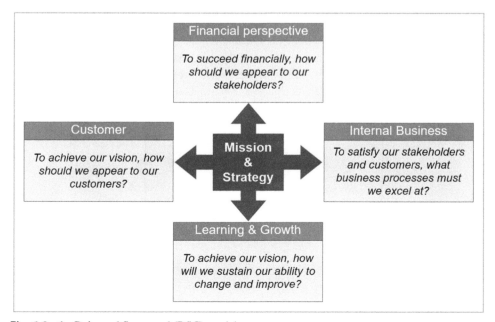

Fig. 6.2 the Balanced Scorecard (BSC) model

In order to understand the concepts, a private company may serve as a reference point. The BSC metrics may include the following items:

Financial perspective
- Revenue
- Expenses
- Net income
- Cash flow
- Asset value

Customer perspective
- Customer satisfaction
- Customer retention
- Market share
- Brand strength
- Customer relation value

Learning & Growth perspective
- Employee satisfaction
- Employee turnover
- Employee skills
- Employee education

Internal process perspective
- Inventory
- Orders
- Resource allocation
- Cycle time
- Quality control

The **EFQM** (European Foundation for Quality Management) **model** has its origin in the quality management and continuous improvement of thought and practices. The framework provides an overall view of an organisation by defining nine factors which drive the performance of an organisation. Five of them are considered to be enablers where the remaining four are results. Fig. 6.3 displays the factors with its relations, Table 6.1 with their weighing.

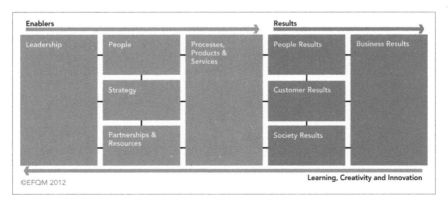

Fig. 6.3 EFQM model

Table 6.1 Factors of the EFQM model and their weights

Enablers (sum = 50%)	Results (sum = 50%)
Leadership (10%)	People results (10%)
People (10%)	Customer results (15%)
Policy & strategy (10%)	Society results (10%)
Partnership & resources (10%)	Key performance results (15%)
Processes (10%)	

6.3   Process KPIs

The BSC framework provides a pattern to identify process KPIs within the four perspectives.

Four examples applied to the processes for IT strategy, IT standards & architecture, IT service and IT project management are show in Tables 6.2, 6.3, 6.4, and 6.5.

Table 6.2 Process KPIs for IT strategy

IT strategy	KPIs	Metrics
Customer benefits	• Strategic orientation	• Contribution to the fulfilment of the enterprise's strategic goals
Financial significance	• Benchmark for IT costs (same industry or type of enterprise)	• Cost-effectiveness (e.g. cost per workstation) • Development of operational and investment costs
Internal processes and quality	• Adherence to goals	• BSC reports
Learning & growth	• Knowledge management	• Availability of critical knowledge

Table 6.3 Process KPIs for IT standards and architecture

IT standards & architecture	KPIs	Metrics
Customer benefits	• Relevance and comprehensiveness of the system architecture	• Degree of IT flexibility
Financial significance	• Technology lifecycle	• Number of applications and reduction in system diversity • Lower operating costs
Internal processes and quality	• Degree of standardisation	• Compliance with IT standards • Number of different devices to cover similar functions
Learning & growth	• Use of IT architecture	• Efficiency gained thanks to IT architecture and standards

Table 6.4 Process KPIs for service management

Service management	KPIs	Metrics
Customer benefits	• Comprehensible and measurable SLAs • Service prioritisation	• Reporting with graphics about service consumption • Customer satisfaction
Financial significance	• Service price reduction per unit	• Trend of prices
Internal processes and quality	• SLA fulfilment	• SLA reporting • Number of SLA violations
Learning & growth	• Bundling of IT services	• Cost transparency

Table 6.5 Process KPIs for project management

Project management	KPIs	Metrics
Customer benefits	• Delivery assessment of the defined project deliverables	• Customer survey with questionnaire
Financial significance	• Adherence to budget	• Comparison of actual costs to project budget
Internal processes and quality	• Adherence to plan	• Delivery date
Learning & growth	• Quality of project execution	• Follow-up project performance report

6.4   Bottom-Up IT Reporting

The bottom-up approach enables to define KPI families for all IT processes defined. Depending on the size of the company and the specificities of the IT in place, it is then possible to define four to five KPIs per process. If, as an example, ten IT processes have been identified, this means that at least 40 KPIs need to be measured and monitored. This is a lot of work, which bears the risk that the information gained is not helpful for managing the IT activities.

Exercises

For some processes listed below, indicate possible KPIs following the BSC pattern:

- IT financial management
- HR management
- IT quality management
- IT project portfolio management
- IT capacity management
- IT continuity management
- IT requirements management
- Account management
- Release management
- Application development
- IT operations

- Incident management
- Problem management
- IT supplier management

The exercise above shows the effort and energy needed for defining KPIs. The answers need to be specific to the requirements of the company and must remain applicable. Time needed to collect and analyse the data must not be underestimated.

Here is a list of more than 100 process KPIs you may find on the web (Table 6.6).

Having all these indicators in place would require a huge amount of time and energy. However the flood of data may impede the decision making process and the management doesn't have so a better chance to steer the IT organisation. This is certainly the main challenge when implementing KPIs.

Table 6.6 Possible process KPIs

Incident management	1.	Total number of incidents logged
	2.	Average time between the occurrence of an incident and its resolution
	3.	First contact resolution rate
	4.	Average queue time of incoming phone calls
	5.	Percentage of calls dropped
	6.	Percentage of outage (unavailability) due to incidents in the IT environment, relative to the service hours
	7.	Number of incidents closed within the allowed duration time-frame, relative to the number of all incidents closed in a given time period
	8.	Average response time (average amount of time between the detection of an incident and the first action taken to repair the incident)
	9.	Average work effort for resolving incidents
	10.	First time resolution rate by category (HW, SW, user data etc.)
	11.	Percentage of incidents assigned wrongly
	12.	User satisfaction once a ticket is closed
	13.	Number of escalations for incidents not resolved in the agreed resolution time
	14.	Agent satisfaction
	15.	Increased satisfaction with incident management on annual customer satisfaction survey
	16.	Number of repetitive incidents
Problem management	17.	Number of problems registered
	18.	Number of problems solved
	19.	Number and percentage of problems with root cause identified
	20.	Number and percentage of problems with workaround available
	21.	Average age of a problem, per business impact
	22.	Percentage of incidents related to (caused by) problems in relation to all incidents in a particular time period
	23.	Update frequency of unresolved problems
	24.	Average amount of time (e.g. in days) between the registration of problems and their closure
	25.	Number of open problems older than 30 days (or any other given time frame) relative to all open problems

(continued)

Table 6.6 (continued)

Service management	26.	Service Level Agreements (SLA) in place or percentage of services covered by SLA
	27.	Number of fully documented SLAs versus the total number of SLAs
	28.	Percentage of delivered services that are not included in the service catalogue
	29.	Customer satisfaction
	30.	Number of complaints received
	31.	Unavailability due to implementation of planned changes, relative to the service hours
	32.	Service availability
	33.	Number of service improvements
	34.	Percentage of service requests resolved within an agreed-upon/acceptable period of time
	35.	Cost of service delivery as defined in SLA based on a set period such as month or quarter
	36.	Downtime – the percentage of the time in which service is available
	37.	Number of outstanding actions against last SLA review
	38.	Percentage reduction in SLA breaches caused by third party support contracts (underpinning contracts)
	39.	Percentage reduction in SLA breaches caused by internal Operational Level Agreements (OLAs)
Change management	40.	Number of changes
	41.	Number of implementations bypassing the change management process
	42.	Closed changes causing new incidents
	43.	Percentage of urgent changes
	44.	Percentage of rejected changes
	45.	Percentage of changes closed before planned end date
	46.	Change backlog growth
IT operations & configuration management	47.	Uptime
	48.	Unplanned unavailability
	49.	Downtimes per PC user
	50.	Production storage
	51.	Bandwidth utilisation
	52.	Number of audits completed
	53.	Number of high risk areas audited per year
	54.	Number of frauds
	55.	Data centre efficiency in terms of energy consumption
	56.	Server capacity utilisation
	57.	Infrastructure expenses
	58.	Percentage of software licenses used
	59.	Percentage of licenses purchased and not accounted for in configuration repository
	60.	Coverage of the configuration management system
	61.	Correctness of device inventory
	62.	Verification frequency of the configuration management data base
	63.	Average age of the software in use
	64.	Percentage of systems (workstations, laptops, servers) with latest antivirus/antispyware signatures

(continued)

Table 6.6 (continued)

Release management	65.	Number of changes pending future system releases (backlog)
	66.	Number of successful changes within a release
	67.	Number of failed changes in a release (percentage of failed changes)
	68.	Number of outages caused by a release
	69.	Number of incidents caused by a release
	70.	Percentage of changes within the release that cause incidents
	71.	Percentage of releases delivered on time for QA / Test
	72.	Percentage of releases delivered on time for production
	73.	Percentage of releases by priority or type
	74.	Release withdraw rate (what percent of releases never go into production?)
	75.	Total release downtime in hours
	76.	Root causes for unplanned release downtime
	77.	Number of untested releases
	78.	Average costs of release
	79.	Average time between urgent releases of software
	80.	Number of release back-outs
Supplier management	81.	Cost competitiveness
	82.	Continuous improvements
	83.	Cost reduction targets
	84.	Contract compliance
	85.	On-time deliveries
	86.	Return rate
	87.	Order accuracy
	88.	Invoicing accuracy
	89.	Technical support assessment
	90.	Customer service assessment
	91.	Performance against Service Level Agreement
Financial management	92.	Adherence to approved budget
	93.	IT savings
	94.	IT expense as a percentage of sales
	95.	IT spend per employee
	96.	IT employees as a percentage of total employees
	97.	Uptime percentage for business critical systems
	98.	TCIT (Total Cost of IT). This includes all costs associated with building, running and operating the IT environment and includes workforce costs, license costs, hardware costs, software costs, systems costs, outsourcing costs, a portion of HR costs, etc. (in other words, more than just the IT budget)
	99.	Formel: $IT\ ROI\ Ratio = Net\ Operating\ Revenue - \dfrac{Total\ Expenses - TCIT}{TCIT}$
	100.	Net Present Value of IT

(continued)

Table 6.6 (continued)

Project management	101. IT projects delivered on budget
	102. IT projects delivered on time
	103. Return on investment
	104. Percentage of cancelled projects
	105. Stakeholder perception of value
	106. Stakeholder participation
	107. Project satisfaction index
HR management	108. Employee Satisfaction
	109. Average number of training days per employee
	110. Staff turnover
	111. Average number of days absent per employee
	112. Retention of key staff

6.5   IT Reporting "Top-Down"

Another way is to start the process with questions from top-down:

- Who are the recipients of the IT reporting?
- Which use does the information have?
- In which frequency the information should be available?
- In which format should the information be published?

With the following definition sheet, a KPI can be developed best (Fig. 6.4). Customer oriented KPIs should be defined in cooperation of customer and IT.

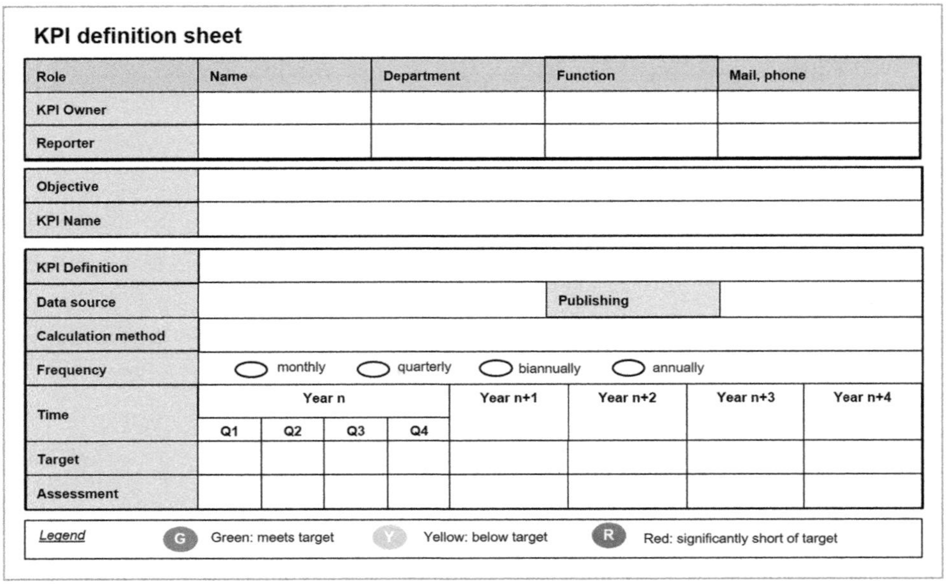

KPI definition sheet

Role	Name	Department	Function	Mail, phone
KPI Owner				
Reporter				

Objective	
KPI Name	

KPI Definition				
Data source		Publishing		
Calculation method				
Frequency	◯ monthly ◯ quarterly ◯ biannually ◯ annually			

Time	Year n				Year n+1	Year n+2	Year n+3	Year n+4
	Q1	Q2	Q3	Q4				
Target								
Assessment								

Legend   **G** Green: meets target   **Y** Yellow: below target   **R** Red: significantly short of target

Fig. 6.4 KPI definition sheet

When KPIs are defined, the reporting pace needs to be set. For a next step, it is assumed that an organisation wants to publish IT reports for the board of the company every quarter. Based on the model presented in this book, IT reporting should answer the following questions for projects, IT services, and other strategic dimension.

Key questions concerning IT reporting on **projects** could be:

- How many projects are running in parallel at the end of the quarter?
- Which ones have been launched in the last quarter and how many have been closed?
- What is the status of each running project?
- How much money is spent on each of the projects?
- How many internal resources are involved in IT projects?
- What are the risks for the company at the project portfolio level and where are the priorities between the different projects?

Let us have a look at the **IT services**. A member of the Board for instance, would be interested in:

- The quality of the services
- The number, nature and impact of service violations
- The measures taken to avoid future incidents
- The satisfaction of the users

Further indicators related to the **strategic dimension** are also relevant:

Human resources
- Employee satisfaction within the IT organisation
- The staff turnover

IT financial management
- Annual budget adherence
- In case, the IT organisation is a profit centre, financial performance

IT quality management
- The degree of compliance of the IT organisation
- Nature and number of outstanding audit issues

Supplier management
- The quality of services delivered by third parties, especially in the context of an outsourcing relationship

IT architecture
- Number of applications and systems
- Number of licences

It appears that a reduced number of well-chosen indicators is enough to govern. These are the so-called "**happy few**" in reference to the St. Crispin's Day speech from William Shakespeare.

Define the content of:

- An IT monthly report
- An IT annual report
- For the discussion of bottom-up and top-down IT-reporting see also Pilorget: "Implementing IT Processes" 2015)

6.6   IT Dashboards

Once the definition of the KPIs that are necessary is clear, it is possible to automate the visualisation of the indicators. Therefore, a so-called **dashboard** should be implemented. In general, a dashboard contains several "widgets", that ensure that several pieces of information are available in a graphical way (Fig. 6.5). A big advantage of this solution is the fact that the updating of the reported data can be realised in "real time", without any extra effort.

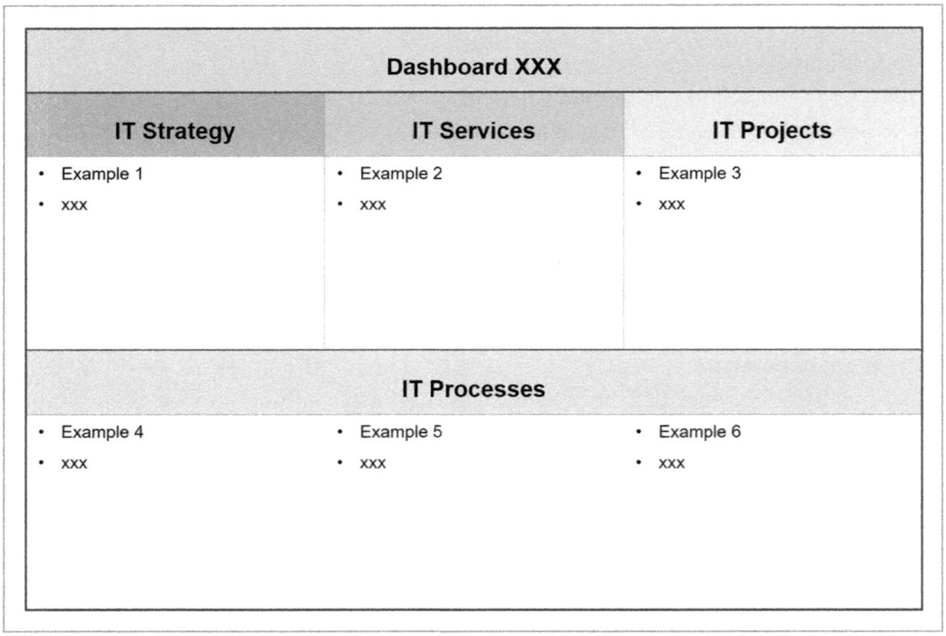

Dashboard XXX		
IT Strategy	**IT Services**	**IT Projects**
• Example 1 • xxx	• Example 2 • xxx	• Example 3 • xxx
IT Processes		
• Example 4 • xxx	• Example 5 • xxx	• Example 6 • xxx

Fig. 6.5 Proposed IT dashboard

Many representations are available and should be chosen in a suitable way:

- **Numbers**
  Graphs are designed according to regular periods of time to visualise evolutions or trends. In certain cases, absolute amounts are needed to check capacity or charging based on quantity levels (for instance 10 USD per ticket for the first thousand tickets and then 15 USD per ticket above). However, pure numbers do not explain enough. They often need to be set into relation to other numbers, e.g. the amount of successfully closed change in relation to the total number (see ratios below).
- **Indexes**
  An index is a measure of price or quantity based on a representative group of individual data points. Indexes are widely used in the financial area, just like the Standard & Poor's 500 index.
- **Percentages**
  Percentages can be used for instance to calculate the distribution of IT investments between the different business units. It is a good idea to standardise ratio and other relations to a percentage value.
- **Rankings**
  A ranking is a list of items sorted according to a system of rating.
  Rankings can be helpful in order to gain a clear view on priorities as only an item can appear at first place.
  While in Australia the ranking of employees ("Employee of the month!") is well spread, this practice is forbidden in other countries. Ranking of people can then be rolled down to team, group or function level.
- **Ratings**
  Position assigned on a scale.
- **Ratios**
  A ratio shows the relative sizes of different values.

In the following graph, a generic structure of an IT dashboard is given.

However, also other structural approaches may be chosen. As an example, you will find a proposal based on the Balanced Scorecard model below (Fig. 6.6).

Depending on the needs of the company, a dashboard can be drafted for the CEO (Fig. 6.7). The different topics collected should reflect the priorities to be addressed.

The CIO is responsible for the correct operation of the IT systems. Hence, focus should be put on incident management and IT operations (sometimes mentioned as "run the company"). But only as a starting point. In parallel, some other indicators should apply to projects ("change the company") (Fig. 6.8).

It is also possible to have dashboards available for the IT customers of the different business areas (Fig. 6.9).

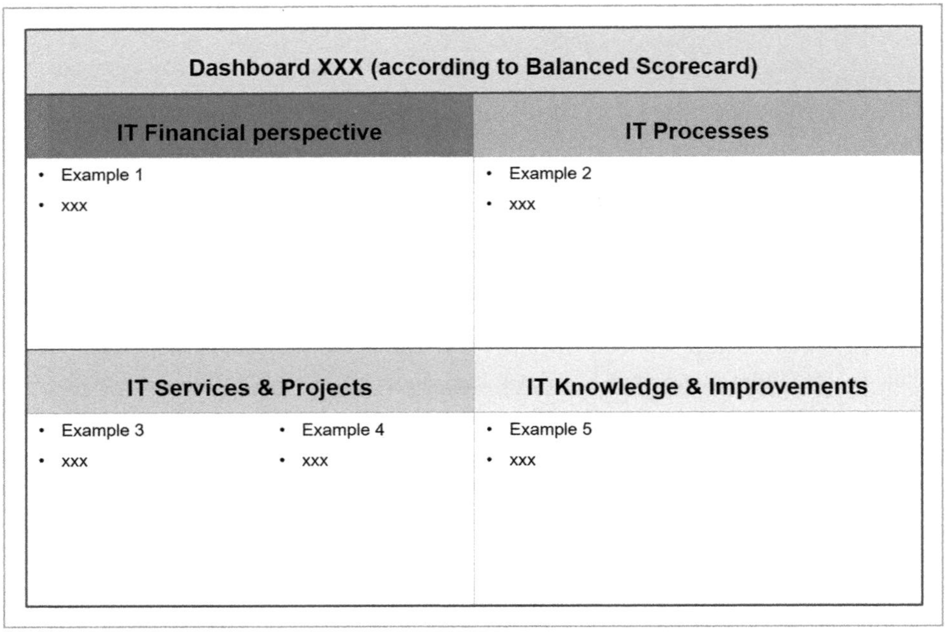

Dashboard XXX (according to Balanced Scorecard)

IT Financial perspective	IT Processes
• Example 1 • xxx	• Example 2 • xxx

IT Services & Projects		IT Knowledge & Improvements
• Example 3 • xxx	• Example 4 • xxx	• Example 5 • xxx

Fig. 6.6 Possible structure of an IT dashboard based on Balanced Scorecard

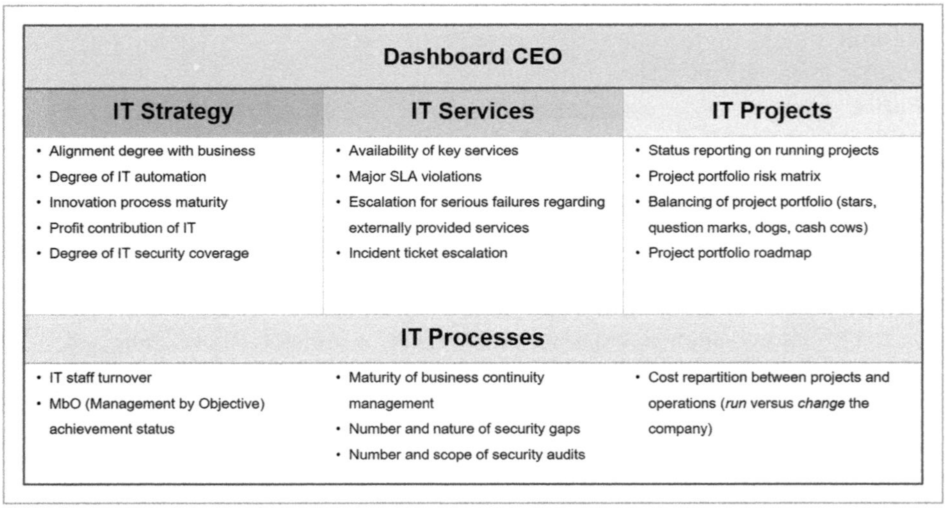

Dashboard CEO

IT Strategy	IT Services	IT Projects
• Alignment degree with business • Degree of IT automation • Innovation process maturity • Profit contribution of IT • Degree of IT security coverage	• Availability of key services • Major SLA violations • Escalation for serious failures regarding externally provided services • Incident ticket escalation	• Status reporting on running projects • Project portfolio risk matrix • Balancing of project portfolio (stars, question marks, dogs, cash cows) • Project portfolio roadmap

IT Processes

• IT staff turnover • MbO (Management by Objective) achievement status	• Maturity of business continuity management • Number and nature of security gaps • Number and scope of security audits	• Cost repartition between projects and operations (*run* versus *change* the company)

Fig. 6.7 IT dashboard for CEO

Dashboard CIO		
IT Strategy	**IT Services**	**IT Projects**
• % IT costs in comparison to company's turnover • Knowledge availability of critical skills • Supplier reliance • Awareness of the IT strategy • Compliance degree concerning IT standards • Satisfaction of IT staff	• Availability of key services • Number of breakdowns and incidents for key services • Reasons for interruption caused by IT or not • User satisfaction concerning IT services	• Number of running IT projects versus number of planned IT projects • Number of running projects in time, in budget, in scope • Cost performance index (forecast versus budget) at portfolio level • Delivery performance index at portfolio level • Business satisfaction of deliverables • Average project duration
IT Processes		
• User satisfaction with Service Desk • Number of major incidents with impact on users and/or customers • Backlog of incident and change tickets • Number of changes and definition of the root causes	• Work load of IT staff • Recording of working hours • Accuracy of SW and HW inventories • Number and fulfilment level of continuity tests	• Number of audit issues or outstanding audit recommendations • Assessment of security leaks • Number of intrusive attacks

Fig. 6.8 IT dashboard for CIO

Dashboard IT Customers (per business area)		
IT Strategy	**IT Services**	**IT Projects**
• Board agreement for new IT investments • IT costs for the business area • IT costs per employee	• Availability of key services • Response time after incidents • Unplanned interrupts • User satisfaction concerning the IT services used	• Number of running IT projects in the business area • Number of running projects in time, in budget, in scope in the business area • Business satisfaction of project deliveries • Business case achievements
IT Processes		
• Service Desk calls for the business area • Number of major incidents with impact on users in the business area • Number of changes and definition of the root causes in the business area	• Testing effort • Continuity fulfilment rate	• SW deployment speed

Fig. 6.9 IT dashboard for IT customers

6.7   IT Budgeting and Controlling

A special topic linked to reporting deals with the financial management.

As many companies struggle with the current economic situation, cost reduction has become a priority for many organisations. Indeed, cost reduction is often the only way to steer and control internal IT organisations. This section will address the implementation of an efficient cost budgeting and controlling (Fig. 6.10).

IT budgeting is the quantification of financial needs for a defined time period, both for IT projects as well as for the operation of IT services, applications, and infrastructure. The time period is most often the calendar year, several organizations have chosen a quarterly budgeting method, the so called rolling forecast. With the calculated demand, the CIO or a defined requester asks the company's decision board or external investors to provide the necessary amount of money for the defined period.

During the defined time period, IT controlling deals then with the supervision and monitoring of costs spent or committed in comparison to the defined budget. Its objective is avoiding over or underspend of the agreed budget. IT controlling can be defined as "*tasks of information acquisition and data collection as basis for decisions of information managers. For this purpose IT controlling applies different approaches and methods, for example, the continuous measuring and interpretation of indicators and characteristic values…*".[1]

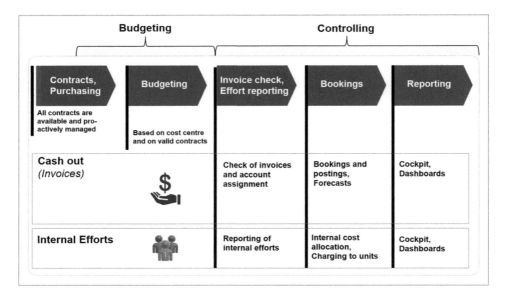

Fig. 6.10   IT cost reporting lifecycle

[1] Source: http://www.igi-global.com/dictionary/it-controlling/15835 from 4th June 2017.

A useful distinction can be made between primary costs (or so-called cash-out) and secondary costs (internal manpower costs).

It is highly recommended to have a review of product and service prices with external suppliers at least once a year in order to adjust the cost baseline. It is a very effective way to reduce cash-out. In most companies, budget figures need to be set by the end of the third quarter or beginning of the fourth quarter. Thus, one should start early to check the relevance of the contracts. The best practice is to check in the time around June. If too many contracts need to be reviewed at the same time, it helps to start with the most critical ones, which most of the time are the most expensive ones.

Concerning the internal manpower, medium-term planning needs to be done showing the evolution of the headcount figures for the three coming years.

Based on existing and valid contracts, services are charged. Invoices need to be controlled and booked on the corresponding accounts. Based on costs already booked, an extrapolation can be calculated. Nevertheless, it is better to estimate a forecast, meaning the projected yearly costs per supplier and per cost centre.

Internal efforts need to be reported and a cost allocation for the corresponding IT services can take place if needed.

IT controlling helps a company to avoid financial wastes and to invest properly. Additionally, the five following measures should leverage the added value of IT (Fig. 6.11):

1. **Optimising the project portfolio**
   Projects should be launched once appropriate conditions are present, especially the business case and the availability of the critical resources. Within the overall portfolio or within special programmes where different projects are bundled, synergies between projects may be used to have the maximal impact of the investments done.

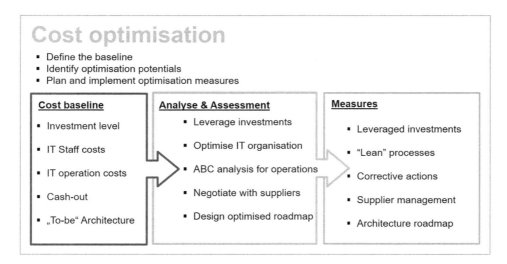

Fig. 6.11 Optimising IT costs

2. **Implementing the right IT organisation**

The IT organisation should be designed to support the long-term strategic aims of the company. It may not be worth putting all energy on the delivery of own IT services if this can be done at a better price by an external partner. One should focus on managing portfolios and planning key activities for the company.

3. **Managing IT operations and services**

Having an effective operation in place where for instance lean management is a major philosophy helps the company to avoid investing extra effort into fixing problems or bugs. Resources can be freed up for new technologies and coming innovations, creating an upward spiral which heightens the interest, motivation and the effectiveness of the IT staff.

4. **Getting the proper suppliers**

External services need to be carefully managed. The value proposition of the supplier needs to be assessed on a regular basis, where market conditions should prevail.

Especially when selecting a new solution, the process, including the request for proposal, should be handled thoroughly and professionally.

5. **Defining and implementing a sustainable IT architecture**

The foundation for the development of the IT systems is based on IT architecture, which is fundamental in order to be in line with corporate strategy and in order to optimise IT costs on the long term.

Literature

Kaplan RS, Norton DP (1996) The balanced scorecard: translating strategy into action. Harvard Business School Press, Boston

Pilorget L (2015) Implementing IT processes. Springer, Wiesbaden

IT Governance

7

Abstract

Leading an IT organisation and organizing the IT activities needed by the business require a healthy ecosystem within a company.

A governance framework is proposed based on Mintzberg's organisational model, which is combined with the design of IT processes where roles are identified. This framework includes three different layers: strategic, tactical and operational.

One of the key findings is the fact that both business functions as well as IT roles are needed to have effective IT processes in place. In this respect the governance components embrace the whole organisation. The quality of the cooperation between IT and the business areas and the degree of integration and mutual understanding determine the potential maturity of the IT processes.

The Human factor also plays an important role in the process of transforming structures and organisations.

7.1 Introduction

The ultimate goal of this book is to find the secret recipe for making IT organisations perform well and even better. While assuming that such a magic recipe can be found, the reality teaches that each organisation is unique and has its own necessities. As mentioned before, the human factor remains the essential success factor but also the main source of uncertainty. However, even if each situation remains unique, the current chapter proposes a framework to understand the roles needed for a good working IT organisation.

© Springer Fachmedien Wiesbaden GmbH, part of Springer Nature 2018
L. Pilorget, T. Schell, *IT Management*,
https://doi.org/10.1007/978-3-658-19309-6_7

A role can be defined as an amount of behaviours, rights, duties, beliefs and competencies enabling to perform tasks successfully in order to execute a process. Implementing roles proves to be a very powerful management instrument as not all situations can be planned in advance. If employees are aware of the roles they have to fulfil, then it may be easy, or at least easier, to master unknown conditions.

Hence, it is essential that employees know the roles in which they perform tasks. The complexity of processes lies in the amount and quality of interactions between the different players. It is possible to transfer this interaction of roles into the image of a football team. A national trainer was asked about the key elements to consider in order to have a national football team ready for the World Cup. He mentioned five main features (Fig. 7.1):

*   **Individual performance**
    All employees are good individually at what they do. Training and coaching need also to be provided. (Efficiency)
*   **Agility**
    People can shortly react to changing conditions and adapt easily.
*   **Quality of interactions**
    Passing the ball between the different departments to offer the best possible services to customers is a great feature of performing organisations. (Effectiveness)
*   **Solidarity**
    It is important that people work for the whole interest of the company and not against each other. It is especially important to keep supportive in difficult times. (Goal orientation)
*   **Role clarity**
    The capacity to interiorise the fundamental meaning of one's role and the expected deliveries is invaluable for the proper development of the company activities.

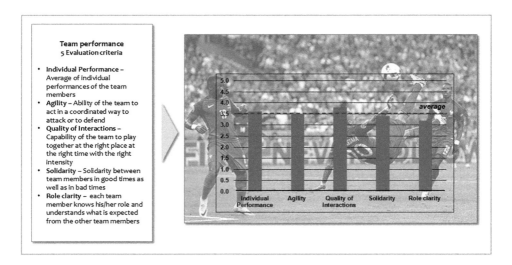

Fig. 7.1   Key features for performant teams

The final aspects enlightened in this chapter deal with soft skills.

The chapter includes the following topics:

- IT roles
- IT governance
- Teamwork and conflict management
- Transforming organisations

The current section aims at:

- Understanding IT roles in an IT organisation
- Determining business roles
- Defining a role-based IT governance
- Knowing techniques to improve team work
- Understanding that conflicts are necessary
- Knowing methods and techniques to solve conflicts
- Behaving as a supportive change agent
- Improving own leadership skills

7.2   IT Roles

Based on the modelling of the IT processes, it is possible to define roles for all process steps. The SIPOC modelling for instance, presented in chapter 2, represents a workable and effective approach to achieve this purpose. Once all processes are designed, all roles needed are identified. It is then possible to create a kind of "reconciliation" of tasks assigned to a single role to gain a complete definition of the corresponding role.

What for example is the role of a CIO? A first approach is to define in which IT process the role "CIO" is needed. It is hard to imagine that the role "CIO" is used within an incident process. One would indeed expect that the CIO role appears within the strategic decision processes. Due to the sourcing strategy, the CIO should also be involved in the IT supply management process. And as mentioned previously, in case of exceptional situations or major service violations, then the upper IT management needs to be implicated.

Depending on the modelling of the different corresponding processes, it is possible to define the role of a CIO as such:

- Defines the IT strategy
- Determines sourcing strategy for IT services
- Defines the IT organisation
- Determines the scope of human resource allocations to the IT organisation
- Ensures that the IT organisation is operational and that its work is aligned to the IT strategy
- Makes sure that the IT strategy is up to date

- Ensures the definition of IT standards
- Establishes the quality standards for the specified IT services
- Ensures compliance with the defined quality standards
- Ensures that the planned IT architecture is delivered according to an approved roadmap
- Ensures the timely delivery of the IT budget and is responsible for adherence to the approved IT budget
- Initiates appropriate measures in response to detected quality deficiencies
- Approves the individual IT investments in consultation with the business management

This principle applies to all roles defined based on a common process modelling.

Exercises

Below a list of process tasks can be seen.

Please indicate which ones are relevant for the three different roles "project manager", "application expert" and "helpdesk agent":

1. Reviews the requirements to ensure their comprehensibility and completeness
2. Takes the role of a consultant
3. Fills out call tickets, provides first aid and closes tickets
4. Is responsible for ensuring the orderly planning and execution of projects
5. Drafts estimates of the associated costs and proposes detailed plans (activities & resource availability)
6. Defines logical data models
7. Receives calls
8. Drafts the specifications
9. Sends regular reports on the status and costs of projects to the IT project portfolio manager
10. Ensures the realisation of the project benefits
11. Programmes or parameterises and completes product tests
12. Provides support when it comes to the execution of integration tests, acceptance tests and training programs
13. Drafts and forwards incident tickets
14. Drafts plausible documentation of project benefits and the solutions that are to be achieved or supported via the given project
15. Documents programmes and configuration elements
16. Forwards requirements questions from incident management to account management
17. Issues accurate and timely reports to the steering committee

The Fig. 7.2 shows a possible definition of roles for a small-sized IT organisation based on the framework presented in this book concerning the three basic elements (IT strategy, IT services and IT projects).

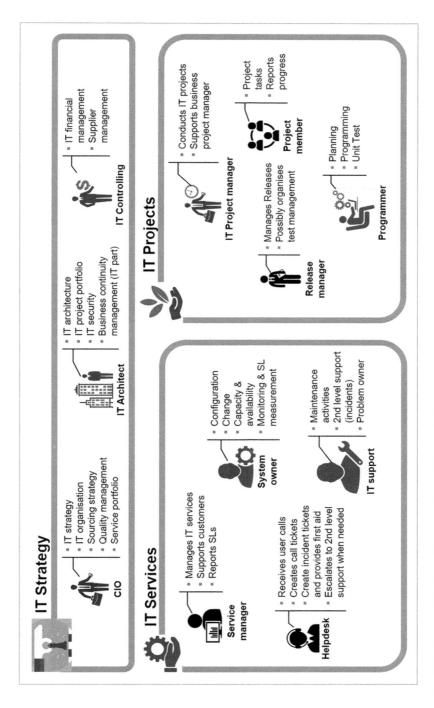

Fig. 7.2 Proposed IT roles within a small-sized IT organisation

In this representation, the CIO with the support of a thin overhead layer composed of an IT architect and IT controlling, deals with the strategic issues of the organisation. Service-related roles focus on "keeping the lights on" and running IT operations whereas the "change-based" roles are in place to manage projects and system releases successfully.

1. How many IT roles are needed to run an IT organisation?
2. Which IT roles do you know in your organisation?
3. How many roles are assigned to you?

7.3   IT Governance

IT governance is defined as a subset discipline of corporate governance. According to the IT Governance Institute, IT governance includes *"… leadership, organizational structures and processes to ensure that the organization's IT sustains and extends the organization's strategies and objectives."*

In order to present a more precise definition of IT governance linked to the modelling of IT processes, a look at Mintzberg's theory on organisations may help (see Mintzberg: "Structure in fives: designing effectie organizations" 1993). Mintzberg's model breaks down the organisation into five generic components, considering the role of each in relation to coordinating its activities. These are (Fig. 7.3):

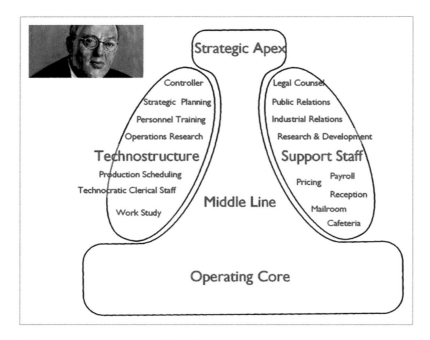

Fig. 7.3 Five generic components of Mintzberg's organisational model

1. Strategic apex
2. Middle line
3. Operating core
4. Technostructure
5. Support staff

Based on Mintzberg's model a simplified organisational representation including four main elements is best practice (Fig. 7.4):

- **Part A: Top management**
  This layer deals with strategic issues
- **Part B: Middle management**
  This part is related to tactical tasks where decisions are made without impacting the long-term future of the company
- **Part C: Employee level**
  This level deals with the "doing" activities
- **Part D: Supporting functions**
  This part includes for instance HR, controlling or auditing mandates

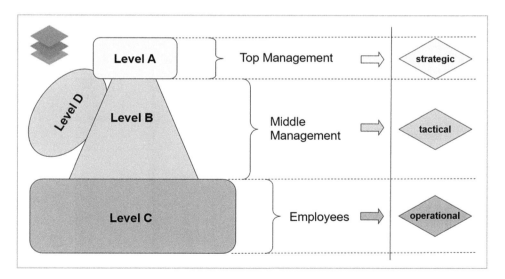

Fig. 7.4 Generic organisational layers (strategic, tactical, operational, support)

Using this structure, it is possible to point out a major challenge of IT organisations. IT services need to be delivered to various internal customers who have very different needs and expectations.

Exercises

List IT customers in your organisation. Give major features for each customer type.
For instance:
R&D

1. Free access to external information brokers
2. Own PC infrastructure
3. Easy search function for document management
4. Highly available laboratory information management system

Controlling department

1. Highly available systems for closing periods
2. Restricted access to financial information …in line with the management competence rules

    …

3. ???
4. ???

The IT organisation must then build "the bridges" between the different stakeholders in order to optimise resources and has to manage 1-to-n relationships (Fig. 7.5).

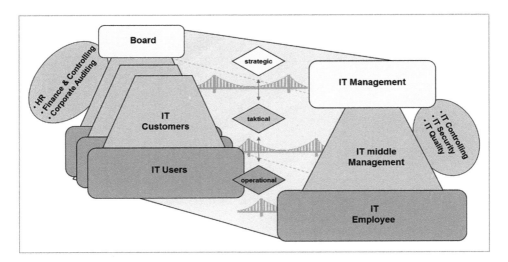

Fig. 7.5 Bridging the business units with the IT organisation

Based on the modelling of the IT processes, it is possible to identify the roles that are necessary in the business as well as the IT area (Figs. 7.6 and 7.7).

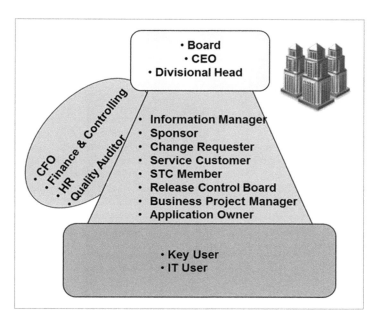

Fig. 7.6 IT Governance – business roles

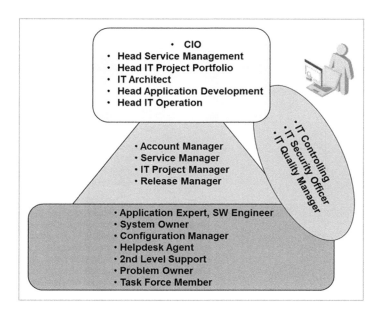

Fig. 7.7 IT Governance – IT roles

As mentioned already, due to the 1-to-n relationship between the IT organisation and the business units, certain business roles, especially at the tactical and operational levels, need to be duplicated throughout the whole company depending on its corporate structure and geographical coverage.

To complete our understanding of the IT governance, it is possible to trace the roles defined in the IT process landscape as shown in Figures 7.8, 7.9, 7.10, and 7.11.

Role	P01	P02	P03	P04	P05	P06	P07	P08	P09	P10	P11	P12	P13	P14	P15	P16	P17
Board	X	X		X		X		X									
CEO		X															
Business unit manager								X									
CFO	X																
Finance & controlling				X		X					X						
HR		X															
Quality auditor					X												

P01 - IT Strategy
P02 - HR Management
P03 - IT Standards & Architecture
P04 - Financial Management
P05 - Quality Management
P06 - IT Project Portfolio Management
P07 - Capacity & Availability Management
P08 - Continuity Management
P09 - Service Management
P10 - Requirements Management
P11 - Project Management
P12 - Release Management
P13 - Applications Development
P14 - IT Operation & Configuration
P15 - Supplier Management
P16 - Incident Management
P17 - Problem Management

Fig. 7.8   Mapping of business strategic roles with IT processes

Role	P01	P02	P03	P04	P05	P06	P07	P08	P09	P10	P11	P12	P13	P14	P15	P16	P17
CIO	X	X	X	X	X	X	X		X						X		
Service manager	X			X	X		X		X					X			
Project portfolio manager	X			X	X	X	X					X					
IT architect	X		X														
Application developer													X				
IT operations manager							X	X	X	X				X	X		X
IT controlling				X		X									X		
Security officer			X				X										
Quality officer					X				X								

P01 - IT Strategy
P02 - HR Management
P03 - IT Standards & Architecture
P04 - Financial Management
P05 - Quality Management
P06 - IT Project Portfolio Management
P07 - Capacity & Availability Management
P08 - Continuity Management
P09 - Service Management
P10 - Requirements Management
P11 - Project Management
P12 - Release Management
P13 - Applications Development
P14 - IT Operation & Configuration
P15 - Supplier Management
P16 - Incident Management
P17 - Problem Management

Fig. 7.9   Mapping of IT strategic roles with IT processes

Role	P01	P02	P03	P04	P05	P06	P07	P08	P09	P10	P11	P12	P13	P14	P15	P16	P17
Information manager						X											
Client						X				X							
Agent									X								
STC											X				X		
RCB												X					
Project manager						X					X						
Application owner										X							
Account manager						X			X	X		X					
Service manager				X					X					X			
IT project manager											X		X	X	X		
Release manager												X	X	X			

P01 - IT Strategy
P02 - HR Management
P03 - IT Standards & Architecture
P04 - Financial Management
P05 - Quality Management
P06 - IT Project Portfolio Management
P07 - Capacity & Availability Management
P08 - Continuity Management
P09 - Service Management
P10 - Requirements Management
P11 - Project Management
P12 - Release Management
P13 - Applications Development
P14 - IT Operation & Configuration
P15 - Supplier Management
P16 - Incident Management
P17 - Problem Management

Fig. 7.10 Mapping of tactical roles (business and IT) with IT processes

Role	P01	P02	P03	P04	P05	P06	P07	P08	P09	P10	P11	P12	P13	P14	P15	P16	P17
Key IT user												X	X				
IT user										X						X	
Application expert										X		X	X				
System owner							X			X	X	X	X	X	X		X
Configuration manager														X			
Help desk agent										X				X		X	
2nd-level support																X	
Problem owner												X					X
Task force member																	X

P01 - IT Strategy
P02 - HR Management
P03 - IT Standards & Architecture
P04 - Financial Management
P05 - Quality Management
P06 - IT Project Portfolio Management
P07 - Capacity & Availability Management
P08 - Continuity Management
P09 - Service Management
P10 - Requirements Management
P11 - Project Management
P12 - Release Management
P13 - Applications Development
P14 - IT Operation & Configuration
P15 - Supplier Management
P16 - Incident Management
P17 - Problem Management

Fig. 7.11 Mapping of operational roles (business and IT) with IT processes

As a summary of a role-based IT governance, the following graph shows the business and IT roles needed for each IT process (Fig. 7.12).

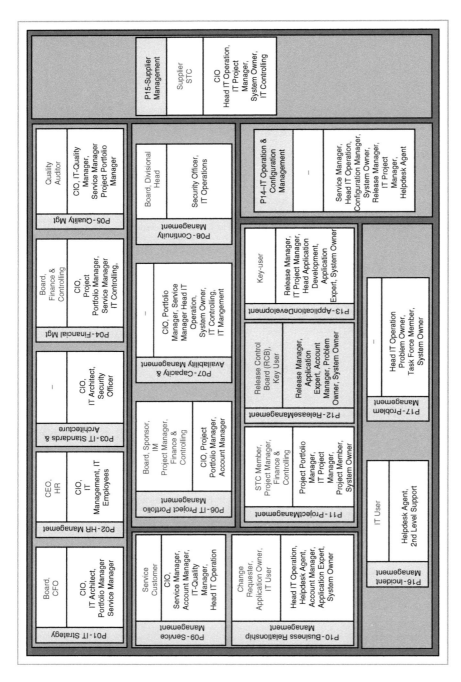

Fig. 7.12 Roles overview on the IT process landscape

It is fact that for nearly all IT processes, both business roles and IT roles are needed. This means that the IT governance is not only a pure "IT issue" but represents a major challenge for the whole organisation. The organisational interfaces between IT and the different units are highly relevant and a good collaboration needs to be nurtured (Fig. 7.13).

Questions

How would you assess the "maturity" of the IT governance in your organisation, especially regarding the following aspects?

1. Are IT processes identified and documented?
2. Are all process roles documented?
3. Is at least one person assigned for each role?
4. Do employees know which roles they have to fulfil (job description)?
5. How many roles are assigned to one employee?
6. Are the appropriate persons found for the role (matching profile)?
7. Are deputies in place?
8. Are counter partners in business known?
9. Are IT suppliers managed?
10. Are outsourcing partners clearly identified?

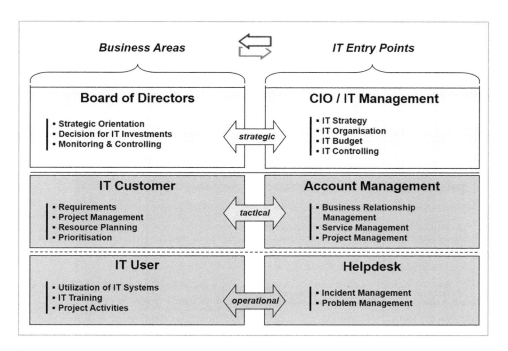

Fig. 7.13 Organisational interfaces between IT and business

7.4   Teamwork and Conflict Management

Teamwork is defined as a collaborative process of working within a group of people in order to achieve a goal. According to the fact that different IT and business roles are needed, it is obvious that teamwork is crucial for the successful completion of an IT project or the delivery of an IT service, as different individual skills are needed to make it happen.

For the creation of "functions" where process tasks can be assigned to, it makes sense to group persons with similar skills and with the same roles into one team.

In general, it is admitted that specific skills and behaviours are required so that effective teamwork can take place. For instance:

- Commitment to the team
- Open communication
- Respect and consideration of the opinion of others
- Support and problem-solving orientation
- Listening and sharing
- Reliability

Questions
1. Which teams do you belong to?
2. Do your teams have specific tasks?
3. How would you assess the quality of teamwork?
4. What are good skills or practices within your teams?
5. What can be improved?
6. Which actions do you take to improve the team spirit?

Building a strong "team spirit" in the organisation is a demanding but very rewarding mission. The challenge consists in each individual in the team adhering to the principles and agreeing to give his or her contribution. Therefore, a vigorous environment is needed to enable learning, accomplishment and growth.

Some "techniques" can be used to foster and strengthen a winning spirit:

- Celebrate successes, also and especially the small ones
- Keep in touch and create "rituals" (in line with the company culture)
- Encourage creativity
- Involve team members in brainstorming sessions for problem solving
- Avoid finger pointing and use "positive feedback" techniques

In 1965 the psychologist Bruce Tuckman came up with the article "Developmental Sequence in Small Groups" where he describes the path that most teams follow on their way to high performance: "forming, storming, norming, performing and adjourning" (Fig. 7.14).

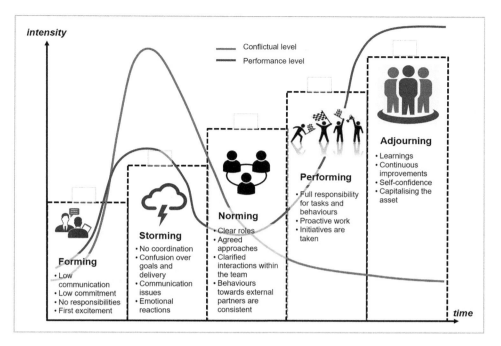

Fig. 7.14 Forming, storming, norming, performing and adjourning

It is interesting to mention that a performing team needs to go through a "storming" phase in order to become a performant team. This means that conflicts are a mandatory element in the process of forming teams. This leads to the next topic: conflict management.

The proposed role-based governance is a powerful instrument to solve conflicts. Indeed, some conflicts are embedded in the very nature of the different roles defined and needed. This approach is especially indicated when "hot" conflicts appear within the team. People may start to speak loudly, be physically aggressive or send incendiary mails. In this situation it is important to explain that challenging questions or critical observations are not meant as personal attacks. Typical situations are for instance:

- The project was very successful and everyone is happy about the end of the project. Now users start utilising the new application and have lots of questions. The helpdesk has to find answers but cannot support much.
- The IT project portfolio manager would like to increase the scope of a project in order to address a recurrent business issue. The project manager is not pleased by the proposed scope increase as resources assigned to the project are very tight.

Questions
1. Describe situations where conflicts appeared
2. What has been done in order to solve them?
3. What would you recommend to do?

4. What about current conflicts?
5. How do you feel about those?

In general, many conflicts persist, especially cold ones, where the situation actually appears "unemotional," but team members act in a passive-aggressive mode. In such situations the question is how to behave. The options are to either being a belligerent to the conflict or an outside observer.

In 1990 Dudley Lynch and Paul L. Kordis published a book called "The Strategy of the Dolphin", where two basic strategies, called the Carp and the Shark, are described. Carps would tend to survive by protecting themselves using a "low risk" strategy whereas a shark is supposed to impose its law on the whole group. The third way however, the so-called Dolphin behaviour, is inspired by the highly intelligent marine mammal. Dolphins are well-known for their agility and their highly developed social behaviour. Moreover, it has been observed in nature that sharks do not attack dolphins in the wild, at least certain species. The dolphin strategy ideally combines high performance with the group identity by encouraging involvement and avoiding single player games.

This simple aquatic metaphor may help to reflect on behaviour and best attitude in conflict situations. Mostly, communication is the best way to resolve conflicts. Hence, good leaders have to search or even force the communication between conflicting persons or teams.

Here to close this section an inspiring proverb:

If you want to go fast, go alone
If you want to go far, go together

7.5   Transforming Organisations

In the former section the importance of teamwork has been portrayed. To achieve a well-functioning team, time and energy are needed.

As Heraclitus, a Greek philosopher, wrote *"change is the only constant in life."* (see "The fragments of Heraclitus" 1889). In the business world one is constantly confronted with strong variable-geometry organisations and volatile or short-term targets.

Change management, meant in this context as organisational change, refers to a significant reshape of a company or an organisation. The Deming cycle, already mentioned in the chapter "Continuous Improvement" above, is a wide-spread management method to develop and operationalise activities in order to take an organisation from one point to another.

Adherence to change represents a major element in the success of a transformation. In an environment where jobs change and where new skills and capabilities must be developed, employees may feel uncertain and behave resistant. It is critical to inform and, as far as possible, to involve the different individuals or groups in order to increase acceptance to the change and adherence to the transformation (Fig. 7.15).

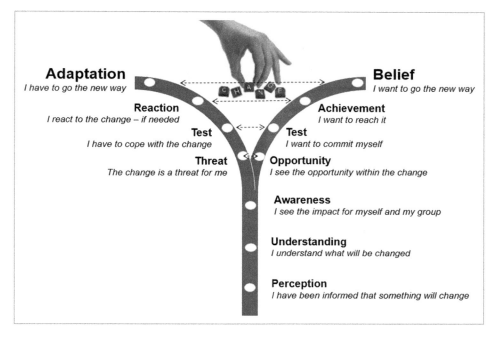

Fig. 7.15   Which change path, adaptation or belief

The **SARAH** model of change defines the stages people go through when facing a change. SARAH is an abbreviation for:

- Shock
- Anger
- Resistance
- Acceptance
- Hope

It is important to acknowledge the emotional component when conducting changes and to release feelings and potential frustration.

Questions
1. Have you ever been involved, directly or indirectly, in a reorganisation?
2. How did you feel about the change?
3. Did you understand the necessity to change?
4. How would you assess the way the change was managed?
5. What can be done better?

Even in difficult economic times, it is possible and may very soon be absolutely elementary to mobilise vital forces of the company to create innovation. The best way to do so is to motivate the staff, especially the valuable staff members. Stimulating motivation is complex as it includes biological, emotional, social and cognitive forces that determine behaviour (Fig. 7.16).

An essential key to corporate success is leadership, which is the ability to lead energies and to steer groups to achieve excellent performance. Being a leader is very exacting as many skills and profound know-how are required:

A leader

- is inspiring
- focuses on team interests and needs
- stimulates work
- motivates
- encourages and supports
- expects the best
- shares a vision
- communicates clearly
- defines clear goals
- gives recognition
- acts as an exemplary reference
- is a person of integrity

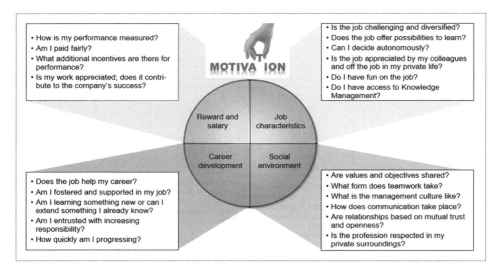

Fig. 7.16 Motivational factors

1. How would you assess your level of leadership?
2. Do you know your own strengths and weaknesses?
3. Can you perform under pressure?
4. Do you understand all important aspects of a task or a project?
5. Do you have a diplomatic authority?
6. Are you sociable and helpful?
7. Do you feel empathy and use it in a positive way?

In 1996 Dan Goleman popularised the idea of "emotional intelligence", as the ability to control our emotions, but also to understand and interpret the emotions of others. One says that the IQ (intellectual quotient) gets you hired and the EQ (emotional quotient) gets you promoted. Socrates's ancient phrase *"know yourself"* is a nice invitation to a reflective journey of understanding and accepting ourselves in order to increase our self-knowledge and to improve the awareness of oneself.

Literature

Deming EW (1982) Out of the crisis. Massachusetts Institute of Technology, Cambridge
Heraclitus (1889) The fragments of Heraclitus (trans: Patrick GTW). Paperback
Lynch D, Kordis PL (1990) Strategy of the dolphin: scoring a win in a chaotic world. Fawcett Colombine, New York
Mintzberg H (1993) Structure in fives: designing effective organizations. Prentice Hall, Englewood Cliffs
Pilorget L (2015) Implementing IT processes. Springer, Wiesbaden

Conclusion

8

Abstract

Is there a secret recipe for a high performing and successful IT?

There is no magic formula that fits every organization. Yet there are "best practices" available and presented in this book, which should be selected and matched to the individual context in which each company operates as well as its sometimes rapidly changing environment.

Major forces related to customers, competitors, compliance and innovation outline the essential contours of the IT organisation and its behaviour.

Nevertheless, key levers need to be put in place and managed to enable a positive evolution.

These are:

- ensure the quality of the IT workforce
- set the right business priorities
- rely on sustainable partners
- explore and adapt

It is impossible to predict the future. Nevertheless, it is important to anticipate future trends in order to keep in touch with the rapid innovation pace most companies are confronted with.

The major challenges can be classified into four categories (Fig. 8.1):

- Compliance
- Customers
- Competitors
- Innovation

© Springer Fachmedien Wiesbaden GmbH, part of Springer Nature 2018
L. Pilorget, T. Schell, *IT Management*,
https://doi.org/10.1007/978-3-658-19309-6_8

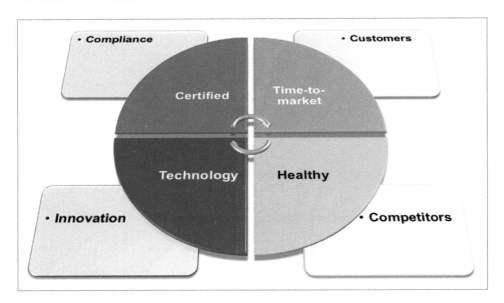

Fig. 8.1 C3I = Compliance, Customers, Competitors and Innovation

Compliance topics are the first priority for many companies. When looking at the banking sector for instance many regulations emerged at the same time aiming at:

1. Enforcing tax compliance and fighting against money laundering
2. Enforcing tax regulation as for example increasing tax transparency and preventing tax avoidance
3. Defining capital and liquidity rules
4. Ensuring that banks have adequate capital at their disposal to cover financial losses during financial crises (Basel III)
5. Protecting consumers
6. Regulating financial markets by increasing transparency and raising investor protection (MIFID II: Markets in Financial Instruments Directive)
7. Regulating banking products
8. Increasing regulatory requirements to control alternative investment funds
9. Imposing main obligations on derivatives market participants including reporting of corresponding trade activities, derivatives clearing via a central counterparty and mitigation for derivatives not cleared via a central counterparty (EMIR: European Market Infrastructure Regulation)
10. Improving risk and data security
11. Specifying the way operational risks in terms of risk appetite and implementation of an internal control system need to be managed by banks
12. Enforcing Reporting and Accounting
13. Defining new financial instruments to enable the measurement of financial assets, financial liabilities and some contracts to buy or sell non-financial items

In many other industries also, new regulations have to be implemented, as this is the case for the pharmaceutical, health, nutrition, and safety sectors.

Questions
1. What are the main regulations your company needs to be compliant with?
2. What is the implementation strategy for these regulations?
3. Which IT systems are impacted?
4. Which degree of compliance maturity has been reached?

Many elements influence the behaviour of **customers** over time. From demographic considerations to the individual hope for personalised services, the range of attempts to predict future buyers' behaviour is wide. Which changes are going to take place once the "digital natives" will own the main purchasing weight?

The online and mobile economy will certainly remain a feature, which gives power to "communities" that assess the quality of a service online and in real time.

In the near future, the availability of services will represent a high need implying immediate reaction times. Client history will be tracked across various purchasing channels. Many of the services will be available in our pocket: shopping, buying a train or a plane ticket will exclusively be conducted with a smart phone. This little device will represent our second brain, as the mouse is the extension of our hand when using a computer.

Within **competitive markets** companies have to stay healthy, especially during economic recessions. In this respect, antitrust and anti-cartel laws have to be functional in order to avoid monopolies and the abuse of monopoly power. Many studies have been conducted to understand how markets work, especially as the transparency between supply and demand is not given. Several factors influence the market laws, like governmental regulations, number of suppliers, prices of related goods, technological development and of course subjective elements like expectations or the fulfilment of expectations. The notion of **ecosystem** is used in comparison to complex natural systems in order to sum up all the interconnections between the different economic actors.

Putting new ideas into practice and introducing new products, services or systems that add value to customers or improve quality can be a definition of **innovation**. Innovation covers many aspects, like:

- **Product innovation**
  Launch of new products or services with added value for the customer
- **Process innovation**
  Implementation of improved production or delivery methods
- **Supply chain innovation**
  Transformations between input products from the market and the delivery of output products to customers
- **Design innovation**
  Enhancements in product design or packaging

1. Which products or services have been launched in your company within the last five years?
2. Does your company have a "product-innovation" (orientation towards customers) or a "process-innovation" (orientation towards products) culture?
3. Who are the innovation enablers in your company?

It is acknowledged that innovation leads to wealth creation. The changing needs of customers, the speed necessary to implement new solutions and the pressure from competitors lead companies to stressing the importance of innovation forces within their organisation. Studies have shown that open organisations ("open" in terms of interactions with universities, suppliers, competitors or research institutes) are more innovative and therefore more performant than self-contained systems. At this stage, the culture of the organisation plays an important role.

The challenges awaiting for companies are multitudinous (Fig. 8.2):

- **Compliance challenges**
  Companies have to fulfil compliance requirements and develop a solid ethic culture.
  E.g. in the banking sector: FING, FIDLEG, EMIR, FATCA, AIA, MIFID, FinfraG, Basel III, IFRS
- **Customer challenges**
  Customers expect super-personalised and digital services usable with a contextual omnipresence and client history across different channels
- **Competitor challenges**
  Companies need to create wealth within international markets with pressure on margins and the development of service packages
- **Innovation challenges**
  Emergence of disruptive technologies like Xml, QR code, Block chain, Artificial Intelligence, DNA App Store, Power from the Air, Conversational Interfaces

As business reality becomes more and more complex and information systems are increasingly interrelated, the handling of IT topics may appear to be contradictory. On the one hand IT is considered to be an enabler to speed-up innovations and enhance new business models. On the other hand, substantial cost reductions in IT are expected. The combination of these opposing forces imposes new constraints on the IT organisation (Fig. 8.3).

One of the remaining questions deals with the identification of the critical success factors, which should enable the IT organisation to deliver added value to the company.

Fig. 8.2 C3I Challenges for companies (C3I = Compliance, Customers, Competitors and Innovation)

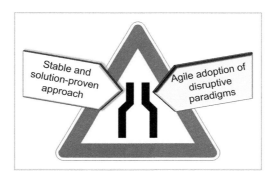

Fig. 8.3 Narrow path for IT between robustness and flexibility

Four major levers have been identified and are proposed (Fig. 8.4).

The first lever deals with the quality of the **IT workforce**. It is most essential to have a highly skilled IT staff and to invest on a regular basis in the continuing education. Some organisations simply hire only "the best". The empowerment and promotion of internal employees should be fostered. The dependency to external consultants should be kept to a minimum.

Setting **the right business priorities** is key for the success of many initiatives. One cannot expect good results with high quality just by giving new requests on top.

In our everyday life the same principle applies with the wardrobe. New beautiful clothes may provide great pleasure. Nevertheless, the size of the wardrobe, in general, remains the same, similar to the amount of the IT resources, which means that some clothes need to be

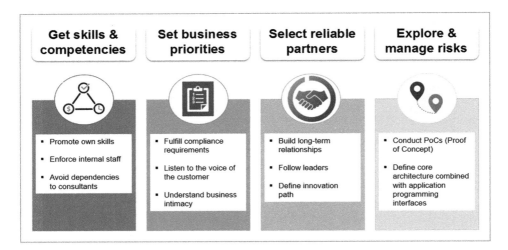

Fig. 8.4 Key levers for a successful IT

recycled. In general, prioritisation of business requirements follows clear prioritisation rules:

- Prio 1: compliance requirements
- Prio 2: strategic corporate requests
- Prio 3: understanding and anticipating market needs

A good understanding of the company strengths and the courage of taking decisions are important entrepreneurial skills.

In order to square the circle, it is important to rely on **sustainable partners** by building long-term relation - or even partnerships. Based on trustful and open exchanges, new technologies and industry standards can be introduced.

The last feature refers to the willingness, and most of the time the necessity, **to explore and adapt**.

The idea is not new. The Prince of Wales made a point in his speech at the British Industries Fair in 1927: *"The young business and professional men of this country must get together round the table, adopt methods that have proved so sound in the past, adapt them to the changing needs of the times and wherever possible, improve them."* The ability to investigate and the disposition to fail and learn enable organisations to progress and develop over decades.

This is the end of this journey. It is up to the reader now to reflect on the framework presented and to draw own conclusions concerning the relevance of the theories exposed. It is still essential to gather knowledge and to promote learnings and information exchanges. This book will not replace individual experience, but it can encourage the reader to extend his or her field of expertise.

Index

© Springer Fachmedien Wiesbaden GmbH, part of Springer Nature 2018
L. Pilorget, T. Schell, *IT Management*,
https://doi.org/10.1007/978-3-658-19309-6